RAILROADED

The True Stories of the First 100 Executions in
Virginia's Electric Chair

Dale M. Brumfield

RICHMOND, VA

HJH Media
Richmond, Va
HJHMedia@mail.com
www.dalebrumfield.net

Front cover: condemned inmate No. 27, Thomas Noel, executed June 10, 1910. Design by Hunter Brumfield. *Photo courtesy Library of Virginia.*

Abbreviated portions of a few of these stories appeared in "Virginia State Penitentiary: A Notorious History (History Press, Charleston, SC., 2017), the Staunton News Leader, and on Medium.com

Railroaded: The True Stories of the First 100 Executions in Virginia's Electric Chair / Dale M. Brumfield. -- 1st ed.

First published 2020.
Manufactured in the United States
ISBN 978-0578720814

Contents

Foreword

I T WOULD HAVE BEEN AN APPROPRIATE SETTING for a Frankenstein remake. This was October 1990, in what was left of the soon-to-be-demolished Virginia State Penitentiary. Following temporary protocol, one death row inmate – almost the only inmate in the entire prison – had been moved from a newer facility in Southside Virginia to spend the last 15 days of his life in this gothic dungeon directly beneath cellblock A.

I was a television reporter for Richmond's NBC affiliate and was experiencing my first death row interview. I don't know if I was somehow expecting more sanitary surroundings, but it was anything but. Staring at the old stained walls with water dripping down, and too conscious of the echoes of our own footsteps, my videographer and I were led to a seat directly in front of a scratched Plexiglas window.

Only when Wilbert Lee Evans and I introduced ourselves and the interview began did I realize this was not what I expected. Like everyone else, I had a vague mental image of condemned prisoners as creepy, Hannibal Lecter-like monsters. That wasn't what I was seeing, though, and it startled me. The person who was calmly answering my questions was a somewhat overweight man with, if anything, a kind expression. Not only did I not expect this, I expected an awkward interview, and this was anything but.

Evans told me how he was sentenced to die for shooting a sheriff's deputy during an escape attempt, which he earnestly explained was an accident. He also told me of the infamous 1984 breakout from death row at Mecklenburg Correctional Facility that held condemned prisoners before their transfer to Richmond two weeks before the "imposition of sentence." He could have been one of the six inmates who escaped, but he wasn't. What he did do, and this was confirmed under oath by corrections officials who were present, was prevent the inmates from injuring twelve officials they took captive during the escape, including a nurse who had been tied to a bed.

Before we parted, Evans asked if he could give me some poems he had written to pass along to a newspaper reporter. I, of course, agreed. Again, not the kind of request I would have expected from a death row inmate.

Evans' heroic actions during the Mecklenburg breakout were not enough to save him from the electric chair. He was executed as scheduled on October 17, 1990. As I watched live coverage outside the prison from my home that evening, an announcer said Evans had requested to speak with a reporter from my station. It was probably me. His request was denied.

The execution was one of the more horrific in the modern era. As reported by the *Virginian-Pilot* newspaper, "When the first 55-second jolt of electricity hit Evans, blood flowed from under the leather death mask, streamed down his chin and soaked his shirt. Bloody froth bubbled on his lower lip. Officials said the chair worked fine – Evans just had a nosebleed when he lunged against the mask."

The accounts we read in this new work by award-winning historian and author Dale Brumfield happened long before Wilbert Evans became the tenth person to be electrocuted in the so-called "modern era" of Virginia's death penalty that began in 1982. They are no less horrifying, but not always because of the method used. Like Evans, most of those who died during the 1908-1920 era detailed in this book were Black, and Brumfield explains in sometimes agonizing detail how Virginia's first 100 electric chair executions could not be divorced from the Jim Crow laws and mindset in effect at that time.

One does not have to be an anti-death penalty activist to feel the horror at what was done to achieve "justice" in an era when lawmen would sometimes sentence condemned prisoners to the chair literally within hours of their trial and justify it with the claim that it prevented lynch mobs from carrying out their own very public retribution.

These are the stories of the first 100 inmates to be put to death in the electric chair following its establishment as Virginia's official form of execution in 1908. Most are quite brief, utilizing as much detail as can be garnered from the occasional eyewitness and newspaper accounts that could not always be bothered with details, particularly when the crime in question was "Black on Black." Finally, now, we can learn at least some of what was once considered too unimportant for us to know, and we can thank Dale Brumfield and his dogged determination in uncovering that which was once considered too inconsequential for the historical record.

Bill Oglesby, August 23, 2020

Bill Oglesby is an associate professor of communications at Virginia Commonwealth University, documentary producer, journalist, public relations consultant, and co-founder of the Richmond Broadcasters Hall of Fame.

Legal Killing by Electricity

Railroaded: The True Stories of the First 100 People Executed in Virginia's Electric Chair

Extra Brutal.

William Kemmler Dies a Terrible Death in the Electric Chair.
The First Shock Did Not Kill Him and a Second and Third Were Applied.
The Autopsy Shows that the Muscles and Brain Were Literally Baked.
Alive Six Minutes After the Current Was Turned On.
A More Revolting Exhibition Than the Inquisition Ever Saw.

- Headlines from the first electric chair execution in New York's Auburn Prison, as reported by the New York World, *Evening Edition, August 6, 1890.*

"There will never be another legal killing by electricity in this or any other country."
-Public Opinion *Magazine, October 1890, quoting the* Boston Globe.

"But for electrocution. I am heartily opposed to it. Progressive it might be, but it strikes me as being the most horrible form of death imaginable. For Virginia's sake I hope this State will never see it.

Hanging is brutal. I know, but it has none of the horror of the death in the electric chair."
-*Dr. W.J. O'Sullivan, Medical-Legal expert of New York.* Richmond Times-Dispatch, *January 12, 1902.*

RICHMOND: a bill to establish a permanent place at the penitentiary for the execution of state felons passed the House. When the bill came before the lower branch of the assembly from the committee on general laws, C.W. Throckmorton (Henrico) offered an amendment to change the method of execution, substituting the electric chair for the gallows, and this bill was embodied in the bill as passed by a vote of 60-19.

-Newport News Daily Press, *February 4, and February 19, 1908.*

"All of the harrowing details which accompany a hanging are missing when the execution is done by electricity. Not even a quiver is seen on the features of the face or on the body of the person who is passing into eternity, and the whole proceeding is marked by such orderliness and decorum that there is nothing revolting about the execution. And there can be no question but that it is a much more humane method. Within a year there have been two bungled hangings in this state, during which the condemned men must have suffered tortures beyond description. On the other hand the electric chair has almost a clean record in this respect. ..."

-Newport News Daily Press, *February 6, 1908.*

"The death penalty by hanging will be abolished in Virginia when the Governor signs the bill that has passed the General Assembly requiring all future executions be conducted at the state penitentiary without publicity, and prescribing the method of executions to be by the electric chair ... Senator Gravatt favored the bill, as a means of eliminating the brutal scenes attending public hangings, and declared that the electric chair was more humane and in line with progress."

-Newport News Daily Press, *March 6, 1908.*

"Superintendent Morgan has not returned yet from Trenton, N. J., where he went to look over plans for installing an electric chair at the penitentiary. He is expected back this afternoon, and will make a report to the board of directors at once."

-Richmond Times-Dispatch, *March 26, 1908.*

"Within the last two years the total number who have perished on the gallows has probably been as large as fifty. In days to come the penitentiary will have all this awful business to contend with; doubtless the change gratifies those sheriffs and town sergeants, whose fee for such work is only $5."

- Newport News Daily Press, *April 12, 1908.*

"The *Times-Dispatch* has long contended that the publicity, the excitement and the general hurrah-and-holiday air attending the old-time hanging were a positive allurement to the negro ... The electric execution wholly does away with that. The time set for turning on the death current is unannounced, the public is rigorously eluded, and the whole affair is conducted with secrecy and mystery, well calculated to inspire terror in the heart of the superstitious African."

-Richmond Times-Dispatch, *October 14, 1908.*

"Death sudden in Electric Chair"
-*Headline for the first electrocution*, Richmond Times-Dispatch, *October 14, 1908*

About this Book

"That [police] officers are far too frequently hasty in taking the life of negro prisoners is only too well known."
-Statement in a writ of error for condemned prisoner Thomas Noel, 1910.

TO BE CLEAR, many of the crimes described in this book are horrendous, and all guilty offenders deserved some form of punishment. It is by no means my intention to declare convicted criminals all innocent, or to downplay the plights of their victims, whom I sympathize with make a concerted effort to acknowledge when appropriate.

Virginia's history is littered with heart-rending stories of violent crimes often committed by marginalized citizens suffering from a variety of personal and social debilities, including mental illness, intellectual disabilities, overwhelming poverty, substance abuse, and domestic violence – issues we see on death rows today. There were no proactive assistance programs or social safety nets for anyone in those days, only reactive criminal justice retribution.

Thanks to the work of organizations such as the Innocence Project, today we know that at least 11 out of every 100 death row prisoners are innocent of the crimes for which they were sentenced to death – and those are the ones fortunate enough to be discovered before execution.

So how many of the 100 people described in this book were innocent of the crimes for which they were executed?

The haphazard, mob violence-driven, racially prejudiced criminal justice procedures of early twentieth-century Jim Crow make this determination impossible. From 1908 to 1920, after a serious crime was committed (or alleged to be committed), suspects were frequently caught not by law enforcement but by hastily-thrown together posses of angry, armed White men consumed with pinning the crime on someone, anyone. Suspects were routinely bullied, beaten, and threatened into confessions. They sometimes had no legal counsel. They cowered in jail cells while lynch mobs outside howled for their heads. Bogus trials sometimes lasted only 20-30 minutes, and jury deliberations were mere formalities, occasionally taking as little as five minutes. There were little to no appeal procedures.

An overwhelming majority of these people were put to death based solely on eyewitness identification, sometimes publicly by young children under enormous pressure to "do the right thing." This practice alone remains a substantial cause of wrongful convictions, even in the twenty-first century. According to the 2017 report "Race and Wrongful Convictions in the United States," the rate of mistaken eyewitness identifications in cases of wrongful sexual assault convictions, is a dumbfounding 79 percent for Black defendants and 51 percent for their White counterparts.

My greatest sadness in preparing this book is the realization that these 100 condemned people and their victims' lives are only defined by a single crime and a punishment. They were fathers, sons, daughters, friends, neighbors, and co-workers. The only attention they drew was when they testified in court, when they were executed, or worse, when a lynch mob was out for them. They deserved more.

Media Bias & Mistakes

"Truth in essentials, imagination in non-essentials, is considered a legitimate rule of action in every office. The paramount objective is to make an interesting story."

- The obligations of professional journalists, as explained in "Practical Journalism: A Complete Manual of the Best Newspaper Methods" by Edwin L. Shuman (1894).

Virginia's death penalty started under Colonial British rule, but accelerated greatly during the Jim Crow era and was hitting its full noxious stride when the electric chair began its odious work in October 1908 in the basement of the Virginia State Penitentiary in Richmond. This was a transformative moment in Virginia criminal justice reform history, and in researching through hundreds of newspapers, penitentiary records, trial transcripts, and gubernatorial papers regarding it, trends emerged, both in the racially biased application of this new form of capital punishment but also in how the press reported it. This in turn presented numerous challenges.

Schuman's insistence on "truth in essentials, imagination in nonessentials" was a fluid, even murky definition, leaving it too often to the journalist to decide what was essential and what wasn't. As a result, many newspaper accounts from this time were subjective, conflicting, and sometimes highly unreliable, so more complete research methods using court documents, governor papers, and transcripts (if available) frequently had to be utilized to distill multiple and sometimes inconsistent accounts to arrive at the most truthful outcome. Sometimes it may or may not be the actual story – which may be lost forever – but the most plausible story that is ultimately presented.

Victims – when named – were almost always misidentified or had their names misspelled. In many cases, Ancestry.com, census websites, and digital databases had better information on the victims to enhance accuracy. For example, one victim referred to as "Ras Nance" in the news was actually named Julia Reece Nance. The press reported she had a son, but census records and her death certificate proved she did not.

Newspapers from this era also routinely published the names of underage rape victims. I have chosen to omit them. Even 100 years later, they and their descendants deserve privacy.

In numerous cases, the newspapers frequently spurned objective journalism to instead speculate on how soon the ill-fated offender would be sentenced to death. Multiple factors, including the races of the defendant and the victim(s), public pressure, and the presence of a competent defense attorney, were the primary drivers behind those assumptions.

Another substantial driver was that the overwhelming majority of newspapers were White-owned, thus exclusively providing a heavily slanted White perspective. Most Virginia-based Black-owned newspapers, which proliferated after the 1866 publication of *The True Southerner*, with almost 50 titles launching, were very short-lived and by 1908, when the electric chair was introduced, there were only three, including the *Norfolk Journal*, the *Charlottesville Messenger*, and the *Richmond Planet*.

While the Black papers like the *Planet* routinely reported lynchings and other extralegal crimes against Blacks, frequently with aggressive editorial comments that "howled loudly, until the American people hear our cries," they rarely reported executions. When they did, the coverage was brief, concise, and strictly objective, with no editorializing on the biased law enforcement methods that sent the victim "to the chair." The *Planet*, which was self-described by Editor John L. Mitchell, Jr. as a "safety-valve for the boiling black protest," with one or two exceptions reported only executions of Richmond residents. The coverage, however, was more detailed than that in the White-owned papers and dispensed of those papers' racist and condescending platitudes.

Of course, many more Black-owned newspapers have launched since then, most notably the *Richmond Afro-American* and the *Richmond Free Press*.

White-on-White

White-on-White capital crimes resulting in an execution were rare, but by far received the most publicity, the majority of it sympathetic and sometimes even fawning. Henry Clay Beattie Jr.'s conviction and execution for the murder of his socialite wife, Louise Wellford Owen Beattie, was breathless front page, above-the-fold news for weeks. Two songs were written about him.

In the case of the "Hillsville massacre," several members of the Allen family killed five people, including a judge, sheriff, and common-wealth's attorney, in a Hillsville courtroom shootout yet they emerged with folk hero status. Many people in that part of Virginia today still venerate Floyd and Claude Allen and their nephews for bravely stand-ing up to what they perceived as corrupt government.

Black-on-White

Black-on-White was by far the most common crime to result in a death sentence. With alarming regularity, young Black men charged with murder, rape, assault, attempting to assault or even just intimi-dating or frightening young White girls, received death sentences.

These crimes received heavy news coverage, frequently on the front page (especially in the locality where the crime occurred) with most of it gratuitously lurid, and often openly malicious toward the defendant. Many articles, almost salivating in anticipation, candidly mused be-fore these trials even began that "the brute" will "most likely get the chair." Less than halfway through the trial of a Black Staunton jail in-mate named Clifton Breckenridge for the attempted assault of a White six-year-old child, his execution became a foregone conclusion. The *Staunton Dispatch* observed that "The expression on the faces of the ju-rors was a visible indication of the fate which awaited the negro."

Not one White defendant was ever referred to by the press as a brute.

Black-on-Black

Executions for Black-on-Black crimes were far less common than Black-on-White, and with a few exceptions received minimal news coverage. To underscore what the White press considered to be the lower-class lifestyles of the Black communities, and to manipulate public opinion against the defendants, descriptions highlighting drunk, depraved, or vicious behavior became a crucial element of the press's coverage to render Black convictions and executions more justifiable to White sensibilities. Herbert Peyton and his victim Cornelius Johnson, for example, were two Black men "stocked up on third-rail whiskey" when they got into a fight. John and William Brown's crime was described as accomplished "with the fiendish cruelty of starving wolves." Virginia Christian's statement to the police was published in stereotype minstrel, or "plantation" Black dialect to highlight her illiteracy and uncultured manner.

Disparaging comments regarding intelligence levels and even "abnormal" head sizes of Black men abounded. The first man to be electrocuted, Henry Smith, was described as "below the average in sense ...". William Finney was considered to be "an idiot."

The electrocutions in these cases were so predictable that after-the-fact, small-point headlines just austerely stated "negro executed," with only a few bland lines of description. Many news briefs of Black-on-Black crimes did not mention the names of victims, and by 1920, most rural Virginia newspapers quit reporting executions of Blacks entirely.

Of these 100 executions, 87 were of Blacks. These Black lives simply didn't matter.

No White-on-Black

The research also revealed egregious racial disparities hidden within the arrest-to-execution criminal justice process at which the biased news coverage only hinted. For many years a Black person was not allowed by law to testify against a White criminal defendant, so crimes such as the rape of a Black woman by a White man were rarely prosecuted, and never resulted in a death sentence since the victim could not testify against her attacker.

As a carryover effect, there was *not one* White-on-Black capital crime punished by execution – and unbelievably, Virginia did not execute a White for killing a Black person until 1997, when Thomas Beavers was executed for the murder of Marguerite Lowery. Five Black men between 1908 and 1920 were executed for robbery, but no Whites. Twenty-four Black men were executed for rape or attempted rape, but not one White.

Out of these 100 cases, 69 of the victims were White, 28 were Black, and 16 the race unknown or unstated.

Confess or be Lynched

Once captured, law enforcement frequently placed these unsuspecting culprits in no-win situations, with disturbingly routine procedures – surround the accused with White police officers, and give them the choice of confessing and pleading for mercy in the courtroom or declaring their innocence and taking their chances with a sham trial and practically guaranteed execution or a lynch mob, which may or may not be present outside the police station.

Of course, that confession, if they chose to offer one or make one up, guilty or not, rarely earned them clemency. Journalists were not allowed in interrogations, so this dilemma was never honestly reported. The progression may be deduced by researchers, however, knowing the police's rush to make an arrest, the fervor of the populace to find and punish a perpetrator, the relative ease of accusing and getting a conviction of a powerless, marginalized Black, and the omnipresent influence of lynch law.

An Alexandria police chief under intense public pressure arrested former State Penitentiary convict Henry Smith for the murder of White Chicago artist Walter Schultz. Smith was an easy mark and was detained in an Alexandria jail cell on a spurious robbery charge for four days with no food or water to extract a confession. He allegedly confessed, implicating three others.

The case became so circumstantial, complicated, and muddied, however, that there is genuine doubt that any of those four men were guilty of anything, much less a murder – but someone by God was going to pay the price, and it was Smith.

And Smith's situation was not unique. Some of these defendants, such as Winston Green, were mentally disabled and could not even read or write, yet were appointed no legal counsel. A few, like Breckenridge, received death sentences based on the testimony or eyewitness identification of a single child.

After the judge in the Pink Barbour trial told the jury they could not sentence Barbour to death if he were proven to be intoxicated at the time of the crime, someone hand-altered the trial transcript to read Barbour was merely "jolly and talkative," and not intoxicated, as several witnesses testified, assuring his death sentence.

Virginia Christian, the lone female to be executed in this era, received a death sentence for killing in self-defense her White employer. In refusing clemency for her, Governor William Hodges Mann stripped away any pretense of racial equity by writing that "Christian's murder of her white employer, Ida Virginia Belote, was the most dastardly in the state's history and that Christian's execution is necessary to ensure public safety ..."

Case closed.

Bill 398

**An Act to Establish a Permanent Place in the State
Penitentiary at Richmond, Virginia for the Execution of
State Felons upon Whom the Death Penalty Has Been
Imposed.**

"A negro likes nothing better than to be the central figure, be it a cake-walk or a hanging."

> -*Virginia State Penitentiary Physician Charles V. Carrington,*
> *1910.*

I N AUGUST 1827, Richmond Virginia's Federal Court under Justice John Marshall tried, convicted, and sentenced to death three Spaniards named Pepe, Couro, and Felix for piracy and murder committed on the brig Crawford, bound from Cuba to New York. After their problematic hanging (two of the three ropes broke and two had to be hung a second time) and burial, a military doctor disinterred the bodies and took them to the Richmond Armory, where they were jolted with "galvanism," or electric current, in the belief they could be shocked back to life. This process had gained worldwide notoriety when described in Mary Shelley's "Frankenstein, or The Modern Prometheus," which was first published only nine years earlier, in 1818, with a second edition in 1823.

Of course, the galvanism failed, the three Spaniards remained dead, and they were reinterred in a single unmarked grave in Richmond's Oregon Hill neighborhood.

Eighty-one years later, Virginia would again turn to electricity not to resuscitate life, but to extinguish it.

Putting an end to Black Salvation

Bill 398, which replaced hanging with the electric chair and centralized state executions in the Virginia State Penitentiary "A" building basement, was sponsored by Henrico County Delegate Charles Throckmorton. The bill cleared the House of Delegates on March 16, 1908, on a vote of 60-19, with the law becoming effective July 1 when signed by Governor Claude Swanson. "Arrangements now are being made for the purchase of the necessary apparatus which, it is understood, will cost $6,500 ($181,155 in 2020 dollars)," reported the April 12, 1908 edition of the *Richmond Times-Dispatch*. "Doubtless a commonwealth can buy electric chairs on credit, or it may be that the Governor will arrange for the deferred payments."

Before the passage of this bill, Virginia executions were conducted by hanging in the jurisdictions where the crime allegedly occurred. It was long believed by nineteenth-century Virginia lawmakers that public hangings had virtue, that they were instructive lessons, and were a deterrent to crime, especially to the Black communities, where a disproportionate number were carried out. But over time, White Virginians began to realize they had no control over these "carnivals of death," where Blacks turned execution days into something they found unsavory, that is, public rituals celebrating Black salvation.

Facing imminent death while standing on the gallows, the young Black condemned prisoner for the first time in his life held a commanding moment in a previously anonymous and subjugated life. He was seen almost as a prophet; his speech, permitted by the Sheriff sometimes for an hour or more, had authority never realized before, even though he had been convicted of a capital crime. Attendees took off from work, and the very presence of Jesus would be displayed in them by shouting, chanting, swaying, and even screaming. Opportunistic vendors frequently hawked watermelon, lemonade, and patent medicine.

The March 26, 1879, *Richmond Dispatch* described condemned prisoners Patrick Smith and Julius Christian standing at the New Kent gallows, looking out at the gathered throng and being "pleased to see the interest they excited."

"Great Lord, look at de people," the article described in minstrel dialect of Smith admiring the fervent crowd of an estimated 2,000 people. "Dey is settin' up in de trees like turkey buzzards."

Thus by 1908 the all-White Virginia Legislature, after being impressed by a flyer handed around by the Adams Electric Company touting their "100% reliable electrocution plant," decided it was time to put an end to these carnivals of death. Virginia then followed New York (1890), Ohio (1896), Massachusetts (1898), and New Jersey (1906) in acquiring an electric chair.

Taming the Miracle of Electricity

While electricity was still a fairly new phenomenon in 1908, especially in the American South, Richmond was ahead of the curve. In 1888 electrical power innovator Frank J. Sprague had developed the Richmond Union Passenger Railway, the first electric streetcar line in the nation. Over the next 20 years, the need for reliable electricity continued to spread throughout the city, and by the mid-1890s a large part of Richmond was electrified. At the same time, however, 96 percent of rural Virginia still sat in the dark.

Electricity had, overall, finally been harnessed. *Harper's New Monthly* magazine proclaimed that the "immeasurable strength" of electricity "for thousands of years had been hidden in the universe, waiting for nineteenth-century man to literally find it."

Among the electrical miracles on display at the 1893 Chicago World's Fair was an original "electric chair" straight out of the death chamber at Sing Sing State Prison in Ossining, New York. Tourists curiously scrutinized the sleek, oddly modern device presented in a pristine exhibition inside the fabled White City. Conversely, a seventeenth-century guillotine was also on display not in the same sterile environs as the electric chair, but outside on the Midway, emphasizing that even with the "destructive machinery of death," mankind had made impeccable technological progress.

Of course, looks could be deceiving. 1893 Fairgoers were dazzled by the chair's cutting-edge technology and genteel display but were most likely not familiar with the horrific execution of William Taylor that July in a similar chair at New York's Auburn Prison. The first jolt of 1,700 volts only stunned Taylor, a 27-year-old Black man, making him lurch and gasp for breath. When a second jolt was dialed up, nothing happened – the generator had shorted out. Guards unstrapped the moaning Taylor and carried him into the cool-down room, where they gave him a shot of morphine and held him while electricians feverishly strung wires from the city's electric plant through a window into the death chamber and connected them to the chair panelboard. Finally, a full hour after the first unsuccessful jolt, Taylor was brought back in, seated and re-strapped, then successfully electrocuted.

Capital punishment methods notwithstanding, comparisons between the backward crudeness of the old ways and the progressively efficient new ways abounded at this fair. In startling contrast to the exhibition's futuristic and aptly-named White City, "authentic" villages from other cultures presented on the old-fashioned Midway were chronologically and cynically arranged to trace the superiority of the more refined and technologically advanced "White" American civilization. These included "living museums" of "primitive" human beings "displayed to fairgoers as objects of anthropological inquiry." Fair organizers imported groups of Samoans, Hawaiians, Algerians,

Dahomeans, and even Native American Indians for the sole purpose of reassuring White Americans of how far they had societally progressed over those vulgar colored "objects."

Prominent racist Georgia matron, lynching advocate and infamous one-day Senator Rebecca Latimer Felton furthered this notion historically by designing for the Chicago Fair a whitewashed tableau of the horrible realities of Southern slavery, choosing to display "the ignorant contented darky – as distinguished from Harriet Beecher Stowe's monstrosities (in the book "Uncle Tom's Cabin)." As the last former slaveholding member of the U.S. Congress, Felton wanted to exhibit what she described as the "true story of slavery," complete with a shack and "real colored folks making mats, shuck collars, and baskets – a woman to spin and card cotton—and another to play banjo and show the actual life of [the] slave—not the Uncle Tom sort."

On a side note, Felton delivered on August 11, 1897, an incendiary speech to the Georgia Agricultural Society near Savannah, warning among other things that White farm wives faced no greater danger than "the threat of black rapists."

"I say lynch," she bellowed to a standing ovation, "a thousand times a week if necessary!"

Accordingly, Alexander Manley, editor of the Black-owned *Wilmington* (North Carolina) *Daily Record* newspaper responded with a fiery editorial of his own innocently titled "Mrs. Felton's Speech." This article, coupled with the withdrawal of Federal troops from Southern cities, resulted in the Wilmington race riot, the only coup d'état in United States history. The massacre killed 100 Black men, women and children and wounded over 250 others.

That same Fall of 1893, not at the White City but at Virginia's State Fair, only a few miles from the penitentiary's "A" basement, White people paid five cents to throw three baseballs at a Black man's head stuck through a hole in a piece of canvas in a game called the "African Dodger." Sociologists, scientists, religious leaders, and politicians all justified the game by reminding Whites that as sub-humans, Blacks didn't mind such humiliations, that they were "less evolved," and had "heavy and massive craniums" that resisted such punishment.

All these fallacies further dehumanized people of color, rendering them unworthy of humane treatment and convincing Whites it was perfectly acceptable to brutalize, lynch, and execute them.

Marching into the Future

Evan F. Morgan, Superintendent of the Virginia State Penitentiary, was aware that New Jersey only recently experienced their first electrocution so he wrote to George Osborne, Superintendent of the State Prison there for advice on getting an electric chair for Virginia. Osborne in turn highly recommended the work of the Adams Company of Trenton, who had installed their chair just three months earlier. Morgan would have preferred to keep the contract local, of course, but he couldn't argue with Adams' practical experience and rave reviews.

Adams quoted a price of $3,700 for installation of an electric chair, with the terms of 1/3 cash with the order, 1/3 upon delivery, $500 when the chair was ready for operation, and the balance payable after the first execution.

The $1,000 appropriated by the General Assembly to purchase an electric chair was not nearly enough, so Governor Claude Swanson and Morgan directed inmates to build a chair in the penitentiary workshop, based on a picture of the one used at Sing Sing prison in New York. They are almost identical.

In addition to wiring the homemade chair, the penitentiary had to upgrade its electrical system. The basic wiring work was performed by Adams, but Morgan indicated in correspondence that Richmond's Winston Electrical Co. "improved on the electrical apparatus" in an unstated manner.

The total cost of the new death chamber was exactly $6,000.00, which included adding nine detention cells and three extra rooms, including a "cool-down" room and a steel plate on which to cool the body of the recently executed prisoner.

1908 electric chair control panel. *Courtesy Alexander McCauley*

Virginia's penitentiary physician, Dr. Charles V. Carrington, preferred the change from hanging to the electric chair because he believed, as did an editor of the *Richmond Times-Dispatch*, that it prevented the gallows from glorifying or creating martyrs of the

condemned, especially within the Black population. In an article titled "The History of Electrocution in the State of Virginia," which
appeared in the November 1910 edition of the *Virginia Medical Semi-
Monthly*, Carrington wrote with repetitive rhetorical flourishes that:

> Hanging was an awful proposition, so horrible in its
> sickening details that one shudders to recall the dan-
> gling, struggling, strangling figure, for death by
> hanging generally meant a matter of fifteen to twenty
> minutes of sickening horrible contortions before the
> subject was pronounced dead. Then the preamble to a
> hanging was of the most trying nature and very often
> tended to make the subject a hero, permitting him to
> address the assembled crowd, forgive his enemies,
> sing some beautiful hymn, like 'Nearer My God, to
> Thee,' which we all have a tender association with, and
> then go off in a blaze of glory. This scene as depicted
> above was actually attractive to certain classes of our
> population ...

Dr. Carrington, by his admission never personally observed a hanging but witnessed 37 electric chair executions before he became
involved in an acrimonious dispute with Morgan and the Penitentiary
Board of Directors allegedly over illegal castrations (deceptively logged
as vasectomies) he performed on inmates as an early form of eugenics.
He was refused entry to the penitentiary and replaced in December
1911 by Dr. Herbert Mann, nephew of the Virginia governor.

The end of public hangings outdoors surrounded by singing and
chanting peers to the switch to electrocution in the electric chair in a
dark penitentiary basement before 12 funereal White men was a para-
dox of civility and racism. The change was considered a victory for
progressive reformers who desired a more civilized form of capital
punishment. It was similarly declared a victory for Jim Crow

segregationists, who wanted to eliminate all forms of Black authority, stop large crowds of Blacks from congregating and partying in public, and to prevent condemned prisoners from being considered victims on their way to "the promised land." Simply, it put White males more in control of the execution process, supplying them even more dominance over the lives – and now deaths – of Black citizens.

This "more civilized" progression from hanging to electrocution had also been highlighted in a 1901 film titled "Execution of Leon Czolgosz with Panorama of Auburn Prison." The film opened with views of Auburn State Prison to set the stage. The scene then cut to a prison interior, as guards removed an uncredited actor portraying Czolgosz from a cell. They entered a death chamber with the chair surrounded by four White guards. One man removed from the chair a lamp board, which had been used to test the power of the dynamo, drawing attention to the modernity of human domination over electricity. Czolgosz – who had killed President William McKinley – is then brought in and strapped into the chair in a clinically austere procedure. Then, over several seconds, three electric charges "jolt" his body. There is no violence, no drama, no burning flesh, and no accidental decapitation or rope break seen sometimes in hangings. Finally, two doctors confirm the prisoner's death, which is in turn announced by the warden. They all turn and smile at the camera, confident of their ingenuity in the delivery of death.

1901 movie audiences had no way of knowing if they were watching an actual electrocution or a staged one, as there were no titles, explanations, or disclaimers. The film did succeed, however, as an advertisement for this relatively new method of capital punishment, which had been advocated and personally financed by the filmmaker himself, Thomas Edison.

The Electric Chair Ushers in the Deadliest 12 Execution Years in Virginia's Twentieth Century

By Virginia law, and because of a strict appellate process, there had to be a gap of at least 30 days between sentencing and execution. After sentencing, the prisoner was required to be in the penitentiary's death chamber at least 15 days before their execution, where he or she remained under watch 24 hours a day. Priests, ministers, or pastors were freely available at all times to the prisoners.

From 1908 until 1920 the procedure on the morning of execution was fixed. According to Superintendent J. B. Wood in a May 16, 1916 letter to Sing Sing Prison, the time of 7:00 a.m. was chosen for electrocutions because that was the time the prison doctor arrived, and that both day and night guards were present in case of any trouble. He added at the end of the letter that "I think a man ought to be electrocuted just as soon as he can be after the time arrives for humanity's sake."

In the death cell, after a healthy breakfast and the last prayer was offered, a member of the death team read to the subject the order of the court for the execution, usually just a few paragraphs in length. With a guard on each side, the prisoner was then quickly marched a short distance into the death chamber to the chair. According to Dr. Carrington, no physical preparation was made to the prisoner for the first several executions. Head-shaving to reduce the fire risk (and further subdue the condemned man) became part of the physical preparation procedure sometime in 1909.

Between 6:00 and 7:00 a.m. the jury of six or more citizens and reporters were brought by invitation of the superintendent into the death chamber, joined by five or six attendants (the death team), the chief electrician, and the penitentiary physician. At first, witnesses stood, then were later seated beside the oak chair placed on a rubber mat. There was at that time no separate room or glass partition separating the witnesses from the prisoner.

The oak chair was equipped with five leather straps and buckles, and an attendant especially chosen for this job fastened the prisoner in. Each arm was strapped to the chair arm, one strap across the chest held the prisoner upright, and each ankle was strapped to a chair leg. At the same time, one attendant fit the headpiece electrode to the head, and another the ankle electrode to the right leg.

A non-flexible headpiece and leg electrode both made of copper and lined with a thick, flat sponge held in place with straps were originally used. A subsequent headpiece and leg electrode designed by Adams Electric and improved by Winston were flexible and adaptable to any size head or leg.

It took about one minute to adjust the straps to the chair, secure the electrodes, and place a mask over the condemned prisoner's face before lowering the headpiece. When all was properly fixed, the attendants stood off to the side and the physician signaled the executioner / electrician, who switched on the current.

Despite the iconic image of a large double-pole switch thrown, the original device used a dial rheostat that resembled a one-handed clock face. Once the warden gave the signal, the executioner dialed up the current to a maximum of 2,200 volts and 10 amps, held for about five seconds. Then over about twelve seconds, the current was dialed back to 200 volts and held for three seconds. Slowly over about twelve seconds again the voltage was carried back to maximum, held there for three seconds, then back again to a minimum over twelve seconds, held for three seconds, then back over twelve seconds to maximum and held for three seconds. After 60 seconds total it was shut down.

The first burst of 2,200 volts paralyzed the prisoner's brain's nerve centers, kicking respiration and heartbeat into survival hyper-over-drive before stopping. The second maximum cycle caused brain death and irreversible organ damage. The body heated to between 138° and 200°F, and the leg blistered.

Superintendent Morgan stated in a March 27, 1909 letter to Adams that the current tended to quickly dry out the sponge and produce a shower of sparks, burning the hair. This may have triggered the practice of shaving the head.

The electrocution atrophied the tendons connecting the muscles at the joints, causing premature rigor mortis and sometimes "freezing" the prisoner in a seated position, even as they were removed from the chair and taken to the cool-down room. Once they were placed on the steel table, team members lowered heavy sandbags on the joints to break them straight, so after cooling they could be placed in a coffin or shipping container, or transported to the Medical College Anatomical Board dissecting lab.

Even today, the Virginia Department of Corrections Operating Execution Manual, known as Procedure 460, revised Feb. 7, 2017, states under section F, "Execution Procedures," section 5b, to "Prepare a minimum of ten (10) sandbags." Then under section G, "Post-Execution Procedures," paragraph 2 clinically states "The body should be placed in a supine position after death by electrocution, using sandbags on the extremities. If necessary, bind the extremities."

The October 8, 1908, *Leavenworth* (Kansas) *Post* wrote that "Autopsies will probably be necessary sequels of the first two or three executions, so that prison officials may ascertain exactly how the chair works and whether its destructiveness may be enhanced."

In the modern era, the only organ that can be donated after electrocution is maybe the eyes, if they don't burst or burn up under the mask. One Virginia General Assemblyman from the 1980s, who also was an undertaker and who prepared several executed subjects for burial, verified that after electrocution the organs were charred beyond recognition.

A Reference from Montgomery Ward

In January 1913, a company in Canton, China called Colonial Stores, identified as "Purveyors and Provision Suppliers," and specializing in "canned goods, dried fruits, wines, spirits, tobaccos and cigars" wrote to Montgomery Ward Company of Chicago, inquiring about the purchase of an electric chair, apparently under the impression they could be purchased by mail order. Montgomery Ward politely referred the official to Superintendent Morgan at the Virginia Penitentiary.

"We have written to the firm of Montgomery Ward & Co. Chicago for information regarding an apparatus for executing criminals by electricity, same as those used in some of the states of America," the letter began:

> They have referred us to write you for information regarding this machine. We have a customer an [sic] high official in Canton who wishes to adopt the same method for this part of the country ... I will be ever so thankful for your kind assistance. Wishing you greater prosperity in 1913 than you have ever had before, I remain yours sincerely,
>
> J. A. Cheong, Manager.

Morgan wrote back with an offer to install a fully operating electrocution plant for $3,000, plus travel expenses of $5 per day back and forth to China. There is no record this transaction ever took place, although paperwork at Rutgers Library and Special Collections indicates Carl F. Adams may have gone to China and personally installed a chair.

Secrecy

The new statute prohibited newspapers from publishing any details of electrocutions – laws still in effect in 2020. Photographs, illustrations, and films of actual electrocutions were expressly forbidden. There was originally no penalty for violation, but the press "observed the spirit of the law, if not the letter, ... For the wholesome effect it will unquestionably have in Virginia."

There are very few eyewitness descriptions of actual electrocutions from this period up to today, and the ones that exist are purposefully vague as to be compliant with the "spirit" of the execution law. There does exist, however, four first-person audio narratives of electric chair executions, one conducted in 1987, two in 1989 and one in 1990, recorded on cassette tape. One of them is the execution of Wilbert Lee Evans, who is mentioned in the foreword of this book, and whose execution is listed by the Death Penalty Information Center as "botched." These recordings are protected by 50-year privacy laws.

Mental illness not exempt from execution

On October 9, 1908, the first Virginian to be sentenced to death in the new electric chair, William Finney, had his death penalty commuted to life in the penitentiary by Governor Claude Swanson. Finney, a Black man, was convicted of assaulting a young White girl in Franklin County, and it was a crime that triggered so much public anger that he had to be transferred to the Roanoke Jail to avoid lynching – a common danger seen throughout this volume. Finney was originally scheduled to be executed on the same day as Winston Green, who was the second person to die in the chair.

While in Roanoke, many people visited Finney, and they all agreed with the Governor's commutation as they were convinced, from Finney's behavior and appearance, that he was, according to the *Roanoke*

Evening News, "an idiot." The judge who presided at the trial, the prosecuting attorney, many officers, and reputable citizens of Franklin County all sent letters to the Governor explaining that Finney "seemed to be entirely lacking in any mental power."

On or around October 14, Finney was granted a commutation, and he was transported to the State Penitentiary in Richmond, where he disappeared from history.

The next year Virginia began executing people believed to be profoundly mentally ill at the time of their crimes and continues to do so today. From 2016 to 2019, a Severe Mental Illness (SMI) exemption bill, designed to exempt severely mentally ill persons from execution in favor of prison terms, repeatedly failed to get out of the Virginia House Courts of Justice Committee. In 2020 the bill passed the Senate but was not acted on in the House of Delegates.

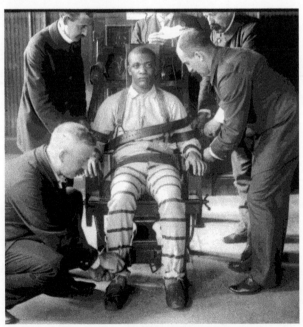

1900 electrocution, Sing Sing Prison.

Capital Punishment in Virginia

A Quick History

"I am well ... I will be electrocuted, whatever that means ... but I wish they would make haste, because I want to get back home."
-Letter from condemned prisoner Benjamin Baily in a letter from death row to his mother, July 24, 1913.

W HILE HENRY SMITH was the first Virginian to be executed in the electric chair in 1908, he was the 1,041st person in Virginia to be put to death by the state. The first was Captain George Kendall, who was executed by firing squad for conspiracy and treason exactly 300 years earlier, in 1608, only one year after the founding of Jamestown. He was buried with full military honors.

The distinction of "first execution" almost went to Kendall's accuser, James Read, a blacksmith who had been convicted of treason before Kendall. In the first recorded case of "prison snitch" tactics, Read saved himself by pointing to Kendall as the ringleader of what was described by Captain John Smith as "a dangerous conspiracy ... for which Captaine Kendall, as principal, was by a Jury condemned, and shot to death."

This act set a precedent that would endure for over 410 years. A 2001 study by the Center on Wrongful Convictions at Northwestern Law School showed that out of 86 wrongful death row convictions, 10 were the result of other prisoners falsely "snitching" to reduce their own punishments.

Kendall was in turn followed by Daniell Frank, who was hanged in 1622 for stealing livestock from a former governor, and Richard Cornish, who in 1624 was hanged for "sodomy and buggery."

The First Woman

Sometime around September of 1630, a married woman named Jane Champion had a brief love affair with another Jamestown colonist named William Gallopin. She soon became pregnant and went to great pains to conceal her very illegal illegitimate pregnancy from the colony. While the exact dates are unclear, sometime in late 1631 into early 1632 Jane gave birth, and she and William allegedly murdered the infant and hid the body. When the crime was discovered they both faced execution.

The minutes of the Jamestown court state, "Wm. Gallopin & Jane Champion wife of Percival Champion Indicted by Gd. Jury for murder & concealing ye death of ye sd. Jane's child supposed to be got by ye sd. Wm. pleaded, found guilty by petty Jury & sentenced to be hang'd."

Jane's hanging is verified as the first woman executed in the new world, and while the record attests that her lover William was sentenced to hang, there is no record that he was.

The next year, on June 24, 1633, another James City County woman named Margaret Hatch was also hanged for killing an illegitimate infant. Hatch initially claimed she was again pregnant to commute her execution, but a "jury of matrons" examined her and concluded she was not.

Some other crimes that could get a colonist executed during the harsh Jamestown laws of Thomas Dale include theft, robbery, "house-breaking," adultery, counterfeiting, piracy, slave revolt, horse stealing (and receiving a stolen horse), stealing hogs (third conviction), arson, poisoning, concealing property to defraud creditors, unseemly speeches and/or traitorous words, bartering with Indians, perjury, and blasphemy. In addition, Virginia imposed the death penalty for many crimes relating to their lucrative tobacco trade, including embezzling or smuggling tobacco, fraudulently delivering tobacco, altering inspected tobacco, and forging inspectors' stamps.

Oyer and Terminer

After 1699, White capital defendants facing a possible death sentence were sent to Jamestown for trial by the General Court. This Court met in various statehouse structures at Jamestown, and the gallows were located nearby. Executions by hanging occurred almost immediately after sentencing by the General Court. There was no "death row" where inmates filed appeals.

Slaves and Free Blacks accused of similar crimes were tried locally on a case-by-case basis by so-called special British-based courts of "Oyer and Terminer" ("Listen and Determine") as organized by the governor. These courts had the authority to reduce a felony to a misdemeanor if the crime was not particularly heinous. Then instead of a death sentence, Black defendants generally received a whipping, branding in the hand with a hot iron, having their ears docked, nailed to the stocks or removed entirely, or other punishment applicable to their specific offense.

The most noteworthy Oyer and Terminer trial concerned a female slave named Eve, who in 1746 was accused in Orange County of poisoning her owner, Peter Montague, with contaminated milk over a several month period. In charge of her own defense, Eve pleaded not guilty, but witnesses were called against her, and the court found her guilty. They then ordered the sheriff to carry out the execution the following Wednesday when Eve was to be "drawn upon a hurdle to the place of execution, and be there burnt at the stake." Burning was a ghastly and excruciating punishment that in England was usually reserved for offenders whose crimes were considered "unusually disruptive of the social order."

The sentence was carried out on a hill adjacent to the old courthouse, and "the smoke of the burning of Eve was reportedly visible over a large extent of countryside." Since as a slave she was property, the court determined her to be worth fifty English pounds, paid to Montague's widow.

As possibly a result of the Eve case, Virginia made it a capital crime for slaves to prepare or administer medicine.

Other notable eighteenth-century Virginia executions include several of Blackbeard's pirates, who in 1720 were "hung in chains" (hanged then bodies displayed in iron cages) in Hampton. Prior to execution, they were held in Virginia's first death row aboard the HMS Pearl.

On November 24, 1738, Anthony Ditmond was hanged near Williamsburg for murder during a robbery. The drop did not kill him, and for three agonizing minutes he flailed in the air, struggling and choking. Starting to panic, the executioner grabbed his legs and pulled to create a stronger downward force. Suddenly the rope snapped, and Ditmond dropped to the ground, stunned but still alive. After retying another rope, Ditmond was executed successfully on the second attempt.

According to the *Virginia Gazette*, Ditmond was "anatomiz'd by the Surgeons." This is most likely the first post-execution autopsy recorded in Virginia.

On March 7, 1752, while standing on the gallows after being sentenced for murder, John Sparks declared that the unnamed man beside him also about to be hanged was innocent. The sheriff removed the rope from his neck and led the accomplice down, his execution canceled. Sparks was then hanged.

In November 1763, an Augusta County judge ordered that a slave named Tom, who had been convicted of murder, "be hanged by the neck until he be dead." Then in a most uncommon and gruesome edict, ordered "that then his head be severed from his body and affixed on a pole on the top of the hill near the road that leads from this Court House ... high enough to be visible from a distance." A slave named Peter had received similar treatment in Orange County 30 years earlier, and for 150 years the area where his head was displayed was known as Negro Head Run.

Killing Children

A Black slave named Clem, who was owned by prominent farmer Hartwell Seat in Surry County, was convicted of murdering two of Hartwell's nine children, nine-year-old Henry and five-year-old Miles Seat. He was convicted and hanged on May 11, 1787. Clem and Hannah Occuish, described as a "retarded" Native American girl who was hanged in New London, Connecticut in 1786 for allegedly killing a six-year-old, are the youngest prisoners to ever be executed in the United States. Both of them were 12 years old.

Since the 1600s, states have executed at least 281 children for crimes committed while they were under the age of 18, and their execution ages range from 12, like Clem and Hannah, to 28. James Arcene, a Cherokee, was hanged in Arkansas in 1885 at age 23 for a crime he allegedly committed when he was 10 (it took law enforcement 13 years to find and convict him).

Sixty-nine percent of these executed juvenile offenders were Black, and 89 percent of their victims were white. Their crimes include arson, bestiality, and theft, but 81 percent were convicted of murder, and 15 percent for rape or assault.

While the ages of most condemned and executed subjects in Virginia from colonial days into the early twentieth century are unknown, a few are verified. In addition to the young slave, Clem, Virginia also executed a 13-year-old slave boy named William [Colston] for arson on September 16, 1796. In 1825, a slave named Isaac [Callerton] was hanged at age 16 for attempted rape. Another slave named Arthur [Clift] was hanged for attempted murder in 1857 when he was 17.

In 1906, 16-year-old Gabriel Battaile was hanged for rape at King George Courthouse. The *Old Dominion Sun* newspaper reported that Battaile calmly smoked a cigarette during the reading of his death warrant, then walked to the scaffold unaided – underscoring Victor Streib's theory in his 1987 paper "Juveniles' Attitudes Toward Their Impending Executions" that children at that age are simply unable to process the finality of their own deaths.

In the electric chair era, the youngest executed was 16-year-old Percy Ellis, who was electrocuted for murder. Winston Green, Arthelius Christian, John Eccles, Harry Sitlington, and Tolson Bailey were all just 17 years of age when they were marched into the State Penitentiary's death chamber. Virginia Christian was sentenced to death when she was 16. She was executed the day after her 17th birthday.

Penal Reform ... Finally

In 1779, Thomas Jefferson's "Bill for Proportioning Crimes and Punishments in Cases Heretofore Capital" was the first proposed revision of the penal laws since the 1611 imposition of Dale's archaic "Divine, Moral and Martial Laws." In this bill, Jefferson proposed that only murder and treason be death penalty-eligible, although he had reluctantly agreed to leave in place certain Old Testament eye-for-an-eye sanctions. For example, rape was punishable by castration, and deadly poisonings were subject to death by poisoning. Jefferson personally despised these ragged remnants of primal codes as "revolting to the humanized feelings of modern times."

The bill failed in post-revolutionary turmoil, then failed again in 1785 by only one vote. Finally, penal reform passed the General Assembly in 1797, with the introduction of the Virginia State Penitentiary system of "labor and confinement." Finally, the only death penalty-eligible crimes were first-degree murder and treason.

As final construction of the Virginia State Penitentiary neared completion in August 1800, a planned revolt led by a slave named Gabriel [Prosser] tested Jefferson's resolve on capital punishment. Gabriel and others had planned a well-coordinated revolt against slave owners and Richmond merchants. The attack—now known as Gabriel's Rebellion—was scheduled for Saturday, August 30, but was aborted by hours-long torrential rain that made roads impassable.

Alerted to the planned insurrection by two slaves who saw the downpours as an omen, the Richmond Light Infantry was called up by Governor James Monroe. Gabriel was captured aboard a ship in Norfolk, and he and 26 co-conspirators were sentenced to death. The hangings began on September 12 and continued intermittently over six weeks. Gabriel was hanged on October 7.

After ten hangings, Governor Monroe wrote to Jefferson, asking if in his opinion more executions were needed to prevent similar rebellions. Concerned that Virginia was appearing to execute out of revenge rather than justice, undoing the reforms he worked so tirelessly for 20 years to promote, Jefferson responded that "there is a strong sentiment that there has been hanging enough. The other states and the world at large will for ever condemn us if we indulge a principle of revenge, or go one step beyond absolute necessity."

On November 11, 1831, Nat Turner was hanged for leading a slave uprising that led to the deaths of at least 57 White men, women, and children in Southampton County. Turner and eighteen cohorts were tried, convicted, and hanged quickly, probably stopping a massacre of hundreds of Blacks by infuriated White mobs.

For Blacks – both slaves and "free negroes" – the laws from this time up to the Civil War became considerably more restrictive due in part to Turner's Rebellion. Under a statute passed in 1848, any offense for which a White could be sentenced to three or more years in prison could result in the death sentence for a Black. Thus, in addition to the crimes punishable by death if committed by free White men, slaves could receive the death penalty for burglary, armed robbery, and kidnapping as well as various other offenses which were no longer capital crimes for anyone else.

From 1800 to 1860, Virginia executed 467 people, with 443 Black and only 24 White. White executions were almost nonexistent in far western Virginia – in 1858 a preacher named Preston Turley was hanged in Charleston (now West Virginia) for murdering his wife. The press reported "the strange spectacle of the execution of a White man in this region. It was the first occurrence of the kind ever known to have taken place within the county." The event was so unique that the *Charleston Star* estimated 5,000 people showed up.

Executions did not slow during the war years, with 46 hangings (all Blacks except for two) between 1860 and 1865. After the conclusion of the war in 1865 until 1908, Virginia picked up the pace, executing 197 people, with 163 Black and 34 White.

The Link to Lynching

"That the murder of Black victims is treated as less culpable than the murder of white victims provides a haunting reminder of once-prevalent Southern lynchings."

- *Supreme Court Justice John Paul Stevens, The New York Review of Books, 2010.*

While 99 men and one woman were legally executed in the Virginia electric chair between 1908 and 1920, there were, according to James Madison University's racial terror website, seven illegal lynchings. This disproportionate comparison highlights Virginia's still-relevant "rocket docket" capital punishment system, which is key in considering the relationship between legal executions and extralegal lynchings in the Old Dominion.

While several factors are considered crucial in Virginia's relatively low lynching numbers during this period, including strong governmental opposition to the practice, the extraordinary speed at which Virginia would arrest, try, convict, sentence then execute overwhelmingly young Black men, almost always for attacking a White person, frequently placated seemingly ever-present lynch mobs. At times, these quickly-formed mobs were repulsed from jail steps by judges and sheriffs who pleaded with them, maybe with a wink and a nod, to quietly disperse and "let the law take its course" – dog-whistle for "let a legal lynching" occur.

The fear of "Judge Lynch" was so pronounced with Virginia legislators that they exploited it to further isolate Blacks and increase the utilization of death sentences. In 1894 the General Assembly authorized the death penalty for Blacks charged with attempted rape "because of fears that failure to do so would risk the lynching of persons accused of that crime." In 1921 this fear was openly admitted in an Augusta County case, Hart v. Commonwealth, which stated:

> The likelihood of the resort to lynch law, unless there
> is a prompt conviction and a severe penalty imposed,
> and thus a resultant grave shock to the peace and dig-
> nity of the Commonwealth, is well known to exist,
> almost, if not quite equally, in the case of an attempted
> as of a consummated rape.

In his 1988 book "Lynching in the New South" historian Fitzhugh Brundage expressed skepticism on whether speedy trials concluding in executions were truly effective in reducing lynchings, but evidence shows that in the first decades of the twentieth century the two co-existed in Virginia (and in many Southern states) for the same reason – to terrorize the Black population with an efficient, guaranteed outcome of guilty and a subsequent quick death. An editorial in the October 14, 1908, *Richmond Times-Dispatch* inadvertently compared the use of the brand-new electric chair and the newly-instituted secrecy surrounding it as almost identical to lynching, in that the chair was "... well calculated to inspire terror in the heart of the superstitious African." Executions were thus carried out in similar manners as lynchings, with the only difference executions were completely lawful.

In these stories of the first 99 men and one woman executed in the electric chair, example after example after example of this "rocket docket" system is on full, racist display. Accused of "criminally assaulting" a six-year-old White girl in Fairfax in 1913, Benjamin Baily was indicted by a special grand jury after only "a few minutes" of deliberation and entered a plea of not guilty. Two days later, Bailey was tried, convicted, and sentenced to die in an absurd two-hour trial with the elementary-aged child the only witness. The jury returned with a death sentence after 12 minutes.

Charles Gillespie was found guilty of "attempted criminal assault" of the 19-year-old daughter of a prominent White businessman at Richmond's Hustings Court on January 16, 1909. The all-White jury sentenced him to death after less than five minutes deliberation under the auspices of "protecting Richmond's womanhood." Gillespie was executed in the electric chair on February 16, a mere 38 days after the attack.

Arthelius "Felix" Christian, a 17-year-old Black teenager, was arrested and charged with assaulting and then stabbing to death a 14-year-old White school girl in Botetourt County in February 1909. As a lynch mob gathered at the Botetourt courthouse, Christian was in-dicted, tried and convicted within 24 hours of his capture. His trial, from the time the sheriff called the court to order until the sentence was pronounced, took only 21 minutes. The February 26, 1909 edition of the *Virginia Citizen* reported in a brief statement on page two that "this was the swiftest meeting [*sic*] out of justice in the history of the criminal courts of Virginia" because (as ominously proven later in Hart v. Commonwealth) "it prevented a threatened lynching." Christian was never appointed a lawyer and was executed only 31 days after his conviction.

When Harry F. Byrd's 1928 law officially outlawed lynching in Vir-ginia, executions filled the vacuum, continuing at a dizzying pace. In the 34 years between the 1928 passage of the lynch law and the 1962 death penalty moratorium, Virginia legally executed 80 Black and 17 White men, most all for murder, robbery, and/or rape of Whites.

Of the 100 people highlighted in this book, at least 16 were terror-ized by actual lynch mobs, with many others threatened with speculative lynching by courts and law enforcement.

The Modern Era

The execution of Carroll Garland in 1962 was notable in that it was the first execution to have a female witness, and the last execution be-fore a moratorium was called. After 54 years of use, there was concern that the electric chair was no longer a legitimate way of administering Virginia's death penalty. A request to appropriate $15,000 to modern-ize the chair stalled pending the decisions of several U.S. Supreme Court cases seeking to abolish the death penalty nationwide as "cruel and unusual punishment" in violation of the Eighth Amendment. Con-sequently, a stay of execution was granted to 14 death row inmates.

In June 1972, the Supreme Court decision Furman v. Georgia em-phasized three inherent problems in state applications of the death penalty: that the death penalty had been inflicted arbitrarily and irrationally; that juries had excessive discretion in determining whether a life sentence or the death penalty should be imposed for certain criminal offenses; and that poor and Black defendants were disproportionate recipients of the penalty.

While Justices Thurgood Marshall and William J. Brennan Jr. asserted that the death penalty itself was unconstitutional, the three other majority justices affirmed that it was not the death penalty, but the arbitrary application of it that was unconstitutional. Thus, the application of the penalty was left to individual states, with several SCOTUS-ordered guidelines.

In an address to a joint session of the 1974 General Assembly, newly elected Governor Mills Godwin called for a resumption of Virginia's death penalty. He declared that a jury should have the option to impose a death sentence under three circumstances: conviction for the murder of a law enforcement officer in the line of duty; conviction of murder in connection with rape and/or arson; and a second conviction for first-degree murder.

Later, in a classic and regretfully predictable slippery slope progression, bills introduced in subsequent General Assembly sessions further expanded the death penalty to include many other convictions, including (according to state codes) " ...willful, deliberate, premeditated killing: In connection with abduction for extortion of money or pecuniary benefit; for hire; committed while confined to state correctional facility; armed robbery; rape, sodomy; law officer or fire marshal for purposes of interfering with official duties; multiple murders; victim in commission of abduction, intended to extort money or for pecuniary benefit; more than one person within a three-year period; in commission of a controlled substance; engaged in a criminal enterprise; outrageously or wantonly vile, horrible or inhuman; continuing serious threat to society; willful killing of a pregnant woman by person who knows woman is pregnant; any person under 14 by a person 21 and older; any judge or substitute judge; witness in a criminal case; act of terrorism."

Where We Are Now

Virginia resumed the same lightning speed of executions in the overhauled electric chair in the penitentiary basement in 1982 with the execution of Frank Coppola.

Coppola's execution did not go as planned. An attorney who was present stated that it took two 55-second jolts of electricity to kill him. The second jolt caught Coppola's head and leg on fire, and smoke reportedly filled the death chamber.

Coppola's backup executioner, Jerry Givens, in a 2018 interview in *Richmond* magazine, claimed his pants leg was not rolled up far enough and caught fire.

Possibly the most notorious execution during this period was that of Linwood Briley. He and his brothers James and Anthony were convicted of monstrous murders around Richmond in 1978 and 1979, and they later engineered the largest breakout from death row in American history.

On October 12, 1984, a crowd of about five hundred demonstrators divided for and against capital punishment gathered outside the penitentiary to await Briley's execution. As a small group of death penalty opponents held a candlelight vigil, across Belvidere Street the mood was appallingly opposite. Many demonstrators held homemade signs displaying sentiments as "Kill the nigger" and "Fry 'em" in a loud beer and Confederate flag–fueled street party. As the crowd chanted "Burn, Briley, Burn," one man commented to a *ThroTTle* magazine journalist that "We think justice today is screwed. Nobody should get appeals … the Confederate flag was from back when we had segregation, not all this integration we have now."

After the execution at 11:05 p.m., the crown drunkenly shouted racial epithets, laughed and flipped middle fingers at the others across the road before they dispersed for a barbeque in Oregon Hill.

In 1991, when the penitentiary was closed and demolished, Death row was moved to Sussex I State Prison near Waverley and the death chamber was moved to Greensville Correctional Center in Jarratt. On January 1, 1995, the condemned inmate had the choice of electrocution or lethal injection, with lethal injection the default if no choice was made. They are also offered a last meal from the prison menu no less than four hours before the execution and allowed to shower two hours before.

In 1994 Governor George Allen signed an executive order allowing murder victim family members to view executions. For privacy reasons, they are seated in a separate room from media and citizen witnesses.

1999 was the top year for executions in this modern era, with 14 lethal injections. Overall, there have been in Virginia 113 executions from 1982 to 2020, second only to Texas, with the racial demographic between men of color and Caucasians disproportionate at a 7-1 ratio.

In 2020, there are only two inmates in a death row that in the 1990s was crammed with over 50. Both of their cases are under review for possible misconduct at the trial stage. More importantly, there have been no executions since William Morva in 2017, and remarkably, no new death sentences have been handed down by a Virginia jury since 2011.

Perhaps Virginia is shedding its obsessions with death.

Electric Chair Checkbook

ACCORDING TO STUBS at the Library of Virginia, a total of 22 checks were written from a dedicated account between June 1, 1908, and March 1, 1909, as payments for the construction of the death chamber and the installation of the electric chair.

Check	Date	To	Expense	Amount
1	June 1, 1908	Supt. Morgan	workmen for week ending May 29	$215.50
2	June 8, 1908	Warner Moore & Co.	Cement	392.90
3	June 8, 1908	Supt. Morgan	expenses to Washington, Trenton & Philadelphia	60.45
4	June 8, 1908	Supt. Morgan	workmen for week ending June 5	11.50
5	No date	Adams Electric Co.	1st & 2nd payment on electrocution plant	2160.00
6	June 29, 1908	W. D. Gunn & Co.	lumber	80.50
7	June 29, 1908	Woodward & Son	lumber	12.50
8	June 29, 1908	C. R. Winston Electrical Co.	services rendered installing electric chair	270.00
9	July 13, 1908	Richmond Iron Works	steel plate (*for cooling executed inmates*)	1.25
10	July 29, 1908	W. R. Fensom	first payment on contract for plumbing	200.00
11	Aug. 10, 1908	Richmond Iron Works	Steel cells (*for "death row"*)	1052.50

12	Aug. 17, 1908	Wm. Northop & H.J. Wickham	Current (*wiring*)	5.00
13	Aug. 31, 1908	Wm. Northop & H.J. Wickham	Current	5.00
14	Aug. 31, 1908	W. R. Fensom	2nd payment on contract for plumbing	203.89
15	Sept. 28, 1908	W. J. Whitehurst	Lumber	29.50
16	Sept. 28, 1908	G. W. Parsons	Doors	35.26
17	Oct. 12, 1908	Adams Electric Co.	Balance due on plant as per contract	540.00
18	Oct. 12, 1908	G. A. Benjamin Co.	Lavatory & bowl	19.00
19	Nov. 23, 1908	Winston Electrical Co.	Balance on contract	623.00
20	Feb. 1, 1909	Richmond Manufacturing Co.	Threshold plates	9.75
21	Feb. 8, 1909	Walford Printing Co.	Electrocution instruction books	17.00
22	Mar. 1, 1909	Supt.	For dep. [illegible]	55.50
			Total	6,000.00

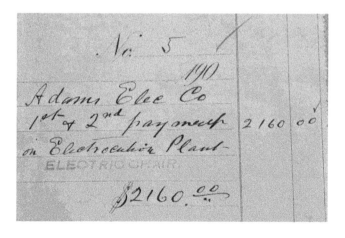

1908

1

Henry Smith

THE FIRST EXECUTION under the new statute of Virginia which substituted electrocution for hanging took place on October 13, 1908, in the basement of "A" building in the Virginia State Penitentiary in Richmond. It was clear to the legislature and the press that the Commonwealth of Virginia had progressed substantially in its effort to carry out the orders of the court in capital crimes "in the most humane manner." Despite some opposition in the General Assembly, those who witnessed hangings had "unhesitatingly declared that electricity was far less barbarous" before even seeing a single electrocution take place.

Penitentiary Superintendent Evan Morgan was overwhelmed with applications to witness the first electric chair execution, but he claimed he had little latitude selecting witnesses, as the law at the time stipulated that only six to twelve White men could witness an electrocution.

Virginia's first victim of this new law was Henry Smith, *alias* Oscar Perry, a Portsmouth Black man. Smith, age 22, described in the press as "below the average in sense but pleasant-faced and seemingly docile," was convicted of raping a 75-year-old White woman, Catherine Powell, on August 11 in the city of Portsmouth. He also robbed her house of $15 and then "beat the old lady into a state of insensibility."

It turned out that as the crime was occurring, a young Black grocery delivery boy named Pope came to the house. "I heard the voice of a woman as if she was praying for mercy," he testified, stating that Powell called to him from an upstairs window to "catch that negro." Running around to the back of the house, Pope testified he saw Smith leave from the kitchen door.

On August 15, as Smith and an alleged accomplice, William "Brack" King sat in the Portsmouth Jail, 14 men stormed it in an attempt to lynch them both. They were unsuccessful, and 10 of the 14, including two Blacks, were charged with rioting and fined $100 each with 60 days in jail. All of those convicted appealed their sentences and were bailed.

Smith pleaded not guilty before Judge Bain on September 8, but Powell positively identified him and described the attack in detail. Smith was then found guilty of first-degree assault, but the jury, after deliberating six hours, could not reach an agreement on punishment, with eight standing for death and four for 20 years imprisonment. After being sent back twice by the judge they finally emerged with a sentence of death.

A juror later revealed that on their third attempt at deliberations, they were told by someone that Smith was a former convict, and had been released from the penitentiary in January 1907. This illicit and uncorroborated information convinced the four holdouts to change their votes.

While in the Portsmouth City Jail, Smith ate constantly. In one note to his jailer, carried to him by a fellow prisoner and trusty named Emmett Murphy, Smith wrote:

> Mr. Hybirt, – Will you please get me 2 scramblet eggs, some cheese, 2 or 3 biskits and a cup of coffee, and oblige, (signed) Henry Smith.

On September 30, Smith confessed to the crime from his cell, declaring that he alone was responsible, exonerating "Brack" King, who was still imprisoned. King was later acquitted in his trial based on Smith's voluntary confession.

On October 1 Smith arrived at death row at the State Penitentiary, and while there he slept and ate constantly. "I never saw a condemned man with such an appetite," a penitentiary officer told a *Roanoke Evening News* reporter on October 6. "The negro does not seem to be worrying about what is going to happen to him Tuesday."

Just days before the execution, Smith's mother sent Superintendent Morgan a handwritten note thanking him in advance for turning the body of her son over to her after the execution. "I was very glad to know that I can get my boy's body by paying all expenses and furnishing coffin so I will come up after him Tuesday. Yours truly, (signed) Pampey Smith."

(For many years, executed prisoners were the only ones whose bodies could be released to families, as long as the family paid the expenses. General population prisoners, as well as unclaimed capital prisoners who died, were automatically sent to the Medical College of Virginia dissecting lab.)

On October 11, Smith confessed in a written statement to R. C. Marshall, Commonwealth's Attorney of Norfolk, that he and a man named Robert Jourdan were responsible for a highway robbery committed the previous year, and that a man named Joseph Smith, who had been convicted and imprisoned for that crime was innocent. "I make this statement of my own free will," Smith wrote, "as I have only a few more days to live and I would not have an innocent man suffer for my crime."

On October 13, the day of execution, the Rev. W. H. Dean, Pastor of Leigh Street Methodist Church, and S. C. Burrell of the Colored Young Men's Christian Association joined Smith in his cell, where they prayed and sang hymns. Smith was then escorted from his cell to the chair at 7:20 a.m. and ten minutes later he was pronounced dead.

There is no record of how the electric chair functioned, as no details were divulged by prison authorities or by the press. Dr. Carrington did praise the new device, writing in the 1908 Penitentiary Annual Report:

> [It was a] swift, sure, solemn and awe-inspiring mode of punishment, and to my mind is infinitely more humane than hanging. Absolutely nothing of the spectacular is permitted in an electrocution, and when you eliminate the psalm-singing-forgiving-your-enemies that usually, I am told, preceded a hanging, and in its stead institute a solemn, very swift mode of inflicting the death penalty, you have taken a step which will in time be powerfully deterrent on the criminal classes.

After the execution, Dr. Carrington autopsied Smith's body and reported that the right side of the prisoner's heart had ruptured due to violent contractions.

2

Winston Green

WINSTON GREEN, a mentally disabled 17-year-old Black teenager, was put to death in the electric chair at 7:30 a.m. on October 30, 1908, for the crime of "attempted criminal assault," or more honestly "scaring a White girl."

On September 11, a 12-year-old White female and two young sisters were driving a small buggy on the main highway in Chesterfield County between Midlothian and Hallsboro when Green and two other Black males stepped in the road, stopped them, held their horse and commanded the girl to get out of the wagon. She got out and Green rushed toward her, but she screamed, forcing Green and his friends into some nearby woods. Several reports, including in the *Richmond Times-Dispatch*, the *Staunton Dispatch*, and the *Newport News Daily Press*, confirmed that Green did not touch the girl.

The girl continued home and told her father what had happened. Furious, he gathered two mobs of 25 men each, and they fanned out in a huge manhunt. After about an hour one group captured Green in those woods. They took him to the girl's house, where she came out on the porch and positively identified him.

A special term of the Chesterfield County Circuit Court was convened within two weeks after the alleged assault, with the girl and her two school-age friends the only witnesses. Though at first Green strenuously denied his guilt, after his conviction he supposedly made a complete confession, possibly in a desperate attempt to avoid electrocution. Regardless, an all-White male jury sentenced him to die on September 20 in the electric chair.

The *Richmond Times-Dispatch* reported, "the negro had no counsel."

The press also reported that "his case caused much excitement in the vicinity, but the jury's verdict was entirely satisfactory to the people." There is no record that the other two accomplices were caught or brought to trial or any explanation of what "entirely satisfactory" meant.

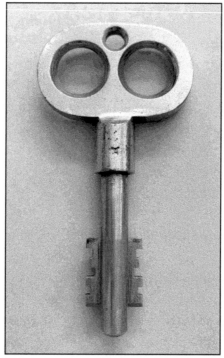

1908 electric chair power on/off key. *Courtesy Library of Virginia.*

On October 18, Green was taken to the penitentiary and placed in solitary confinement in the cell that the previous day had been vacated by his predecessor Henry Smith. He was allowed only pastors for visitors, and even his immediate family was not allowed to visit to say goodbye until the day before he died. Presented with a petition from the family and many of Green's neighbors, Governor Claude Swanson declined to interfere in the case, as it did not contain the endorsement of any court officials or the jury who returned the verdict.

Since Green had no attorney, they most likely had no idea how to do that.

After Superintendent Morgan, who was solely in charge of the execution arrangements, read the death warrant, Green was accompanied in his walk to the death chamber by two local unnamed Black ministers. Green entered the chamber at 7:29 a.m., and in a few minutes, he was electrocuted, removed from the death chair, placed on the cooling table, and crushed flat with sandbags. The body was then turned over to his father for burial.

The press reported proudly that "The infliction of this death penalty was a complete success, with no impediment, and the electric chair performed wonderfully, even better than on the first test a few weeks earlier on the prisoner Smith."

1909

Joel Payne:

Last Virginia Execution by Hanging

I N A SMALL BUILDING in the rear of the Bedford City courthouse, the last execution by hanging in Virginia occurred on April 9, 1909, when Joel Payne, described by the press as "a negro of unusual intelligence," was hanged for the February 1907 murder of his father-in-law, Reed Swain. Payne was hanged instead of electrocuted since he was convicted before the change in execution methods.

Payne had been arrested on July 25, 1908, in Washington D.C. by Detective W. D. Baldwin and two local officers. Shortly after the murder, Payne left and began a job in Silver Spring, Maryland. He later wrote to his wife back in Bedford County, inviting her and their seven-year-old son to visit him. Somehow, the detective heard of the trip.

Baldwin and his men clandestinely rode on the train with Payne's wife and son, arriving late at night. The woman and young boy remained in the station under surveillance by Baldwin and his detectives, and the next morning they were joined by her husband. The press reported that "The demonstration of affection between Payne and his wife and son almost softened the hearts of the officers," but they quickly got serious, and soon had Payne in custody.

He was returned, tried in Bedford County, and found guilty of first-degree murder, despite repeated claims of self-defense.

Shortly after 6:00 a.m. on April 9, Payne, accompanied by deputies, left the jail and walked the short distance to the scaffold "with courage and calmness," with the press describing that he at no time exhibited "the slightest weakness."

Like the condemned prisoners of the nineteenth century, Payne took advantage of the sheriff's situational generosity. He stopped at the foot of the gallows, turned, and admonished the hundreds of people who gathered to watch to lead lives of "virtue and uprightness." He encouraged those who were married or were contemplating marriage to make a home for themselves, "and never live with your father-in-law."

He then ascended the scaffold and in full view of the noose and the coffin, spoke again, claiming that while he acted in self-defense, he was regretful and was confident of divine forgiveness.

He then led the crowd singing "Nearer my God to thee" and was joined in prayer by his spiritual guide, Reverend Blake.

The comparison between this method of public execution and the solemn secrecy of the penitentiary basement electric chair could not be any more stark.

At 6:40 a.m. Constable Mutter hooded Payne and sprung the trap. After 18 minutes, he was declared dead, but his body remained suspended for another half hour. He was finally taken down and placed on an east-bound train to the University of Virginia Medical School in Charlottesville for dissection.

3

Frank Davenport

NORTHUMBERLAND NATIVE Frank Davenport, a 20-year-old Black man, who in November 1908 stabbed to death John Taylor, a "reputable colored man in Norfolk County" aboard the fishing steamer E. Warren Reed, was put to death in the electric chair January 4, 1909.

Davenport and Taylor were employed on the Reed which on the day of the murder was berthed at Colona's Marine Railway in Norfolk. Evidence presented at the trial showed that Davenport was angry at Taylor after being repeatedly teased by him regarding some unknown matter, and twice during the day attempted to force a fight with his tormenter. Both times, however, he was stopped by officers of the ship.

After one particularly ugly outbreak, Davenport allegedly wrenched himself away from the grasp of another sailor and in a furious rush to Taylor, plunged a knife into his chest, cutting two ribs in two. Taylor died a few hours later, and his body was taken to his home in Avalon for interment.

Davenport was prosecuted by Lancaster County prosecutor T. J. Downing, found guilty of first-degree murder, and sentenced to death in the Norfolk County Circuit Court. A motion to set aside the verdict made by his attorney Harry McCoy was overruled.

On the morning of the execution, Davenport was accompanied by two preachers to the death chamber. Despite receiving many requests to witness, Superintendent Morgan summoned only members of the jury, some local surgeons, and some penitentiary officials, including Dr. Carrington. The exact time and circumstances of the execution were not divulged.

Being a Black-on-Black crime, the murder, trial, and execution received scant attention in the press.

Just after the Davenport execution, Washington State Penitentiary Superintendent C. E. Reed inquired to Superintendent Morgan of the efficacy of electrocution and the costs involved. In a January 7 response, Morgan wrote that "... I want to say that I agree with you entirely as to execution by electricity. We have had three at this institution without a single hitch, and have had no outside help at all since the first electrocution."

4

Charles Gillespie

ON FEBRUARY 18, 1909, a described "burly 24-year-old negro" named Charles Gillespie was put to death for attacking 19-year-old Marie Louise Stumpf, daughter of E.A. Stumpf, a Richmond brewer considered a prominent citizen.

The crime was considered by the court as an attack against the "very womanhood of Richmond."

On January 10, Gillespie assaulted and robbed Stumpf at 6:30 a.m. while she was on her way to morning Mass at Richmond's Catholic Cathedral at Laurel Street and Park Avenue. Gillespie reportedly emerged from an alley on First Street between Grace and Broad Streets, demanding money. She gave him 15 cents and a ring, but he allegedly began striking her several times, "raining blows on her face" before dragging her into the alley. Despite being knocked down, Stumpf got up and "fought for her life" while trying to escape. When she screamed, Gillespie reportedly pulled a knife and threatened to cut her throat.

At that time, a man named Irvin Pool, who was escorting a young female telephone operator named Blanche Anderson to her job, heard the screams and rushed to the alley.

Seeing Pool and Anderson approaching, Gillespie fled. Stumpf reportedly fainted, and they carried her to a nearby residence to recover before she was later taken home. The *Alexandria Gazette* speculated that Pool's timely arrival "saved her from awful mistreatment," or rape.

The *Newport News Daily Press* reported that "Dr. W. T. Oppenheimer, who was called to treat Stumpf, stated that the victim bore every mark of a most fiendish assault." One news report claimed she had been "bitten numerous times about the face," but this isolated assertion may have been an attempt to make Gillespie appear even more savage.

About two hours after the attack, two detectives named Flournoy and Miller saw a Black man partially matching Gillespie's description getting his shoes shined at the corner of Beech and Main Streets. After being arrested and searched, the ring belonging to the victim was reportedly found in his possession, as were several articles that had recently been reported stolen from nearby homes. Gillespie claimed that he had no idea where the ring came from. He was taken to city lockup.

As news of the assault spread throughout the neighborhood later that day, a lynch mob gathered outside the Richmond police station clamoring to release Gillespie to them. A Circuit Court judge named Witte arrived in person at the station, however, and assured the mob that Gillespie would receive a speedy trial, and that he would summon a special grand jury to indict him as soon as Miss Stumpf was allowed by physicians to testify. That assurance mollified the crowd and it dispersed.

Public opinion and especially press reports were overwhelmingly ruthless toward Gillespie and sympathetic to the young White female victim, the innocent daughter of a successful and influential businessman on her way to Sunday Mass. Thus, Gillespie's guilt and death sentence were automatic.

The media sentenced Gillespie to death before the trial was even scheduled – the January 15, 1909, *Newport News Daily Press* proclaimed that "The little chance that Charles Gillespie had to escape the electric chair for his crime of last Sunday morning died this morning when the special grand jury met to indict him [for highway robbery and attempted criminal assault], and he was identified beyond all doubt."

The story later stressed the importance of this case and how it had to set an example to protect the virtues of the city's young White women from the attacks of such renegade "negro brutes." Echoing the race-baiting words of Rebecca Lattimer-Felton 15 years earlier, the judge characterized the offense as a "crime against the very woman-hood of the city," and that it was of "vast importance" that justice was served (or more truthfully, an execution take place). The article went on to predict not that Gillespie would be found guilty or innocent, but that he would be executed on February 17. As it turned out, the paper missed the date by a single day.

On January 16, Gillespie – who was represented by court-appointed attorney Colonel A. M. Spottswood – was found guilty of attempted criminal assault by a jury at Hustings Court after an all-day trial, where a total of 40 witnesses, including Stumpf, were called to testify. The *Richmond Times-Dispatch* reported that "Miss Stumpf's recital of her experience ... moved all present to tears."

The January 19, 1909, *Staunton Dispatch News*, along with many other papers, reported "The jury was out less than five minutes."

The *Times-Dispatch* observed that Gillespie displayed no emotion at any time during his arrest and trial. He "heard his condemnation to die in the electric chair with the same air of imperturbility [sic] he had evinced since his incarceration."

There were no appeals, and Charles Gillespie was executed a mere 36 days after the attack.

5

Benjamin Gilbert

ENJAMIN GILBERT, 19 years of age, became Virginia's first White victim of the electric chair when he was electrocuted on March 29, 1909, after being convicted for the murder of his former girlfriend, Amanda Morse, who had "spurned him for the attentions of other young men." Gilbert shot Morse to death on Campostella Bridge in Norfolk on July 23, 1908.

That night Morse and several young friends were hanging out on the bridge when Gilbert approached. He asked the girl in the company of her escort, W. G. Mitchell, to speak to him in private. She replied that if he had anything to say to her, he could say it in front of the others.

When Gilbert failed to respond, Morse took the arm of Mitchell and turned away. Gilbert then produced a pistol, aimed and fired three times, hitting Morse twice in the back and grazing Mitchell's coat.

The shootings attracted a crowd, and the *Newport News Daily Press* reported that Gilbert would have been "beaten to a pulp" had it not been for the prompt arrival of the police.

Hearing from a neighbor that Gilbert had threatened to kill his daughter, T. O. Morse, father of the girl, went to look for Gilbert and reason with him. Morse missed Gilbert, however, and 20 minutes later, while still searching for him and his daughter, was told by someone that she had been shot on the bridge. The distraught father rushed to the scene, and as the *Daily Press* reported, "the fact that he could find no one to furnish him with a pistol was all that prevented a double tragedy."

Gilbert's defense in the Norfolk Corporation Court was general mental irresponsibility, depravity, and hereditary insanity. Upon his sentencing to death by Judge Hanckel, Gilbert simply replied "It suits me."

Following the trial, eight members of the jury signed a petition asking the governor to commute Gilbert's sentence to life imprisonment.

Later, another petition from Norfolk gathered an additional 5,000 signatures.

Gilbert's parents exhausted all their savings to save their son's life, even mortgaging their house to raise money to appeal his case. Gilbert's attorney, Daniel Coleman Jr., not only worked the case pro bono but personally supplemented the money raised by Gilbert's parents to appeal their son's case. Every possible resource was thrown behind saving Gilbert's life, with his parents and attorney fighting up to the night before his execution.

Governor Swanson dutifully considered the petitions for commutation, even granting a two-week respite, but then oddly announced that if he commuted Gilbert's sentence, he could not allow another person to be electrocuted while he was governor of Virginia.

Gilbert went to the chair "praying for the welfare of his aging mother."

After the execution, Dr. J. P. Jackson of South Norfolk proposed to revive Gilbert with a respirator he invented that he claimed could restore life if used immediately after death by electrocution or asphyxiation. The idea was abandoned because apparently, too much time had elapsed between Gilbert's execution and his body's subsequent delivery to Norfolk. Dr. Jackson told the *Norfolk Ledger-Star* that if he could have had the respirator in Richmond, he would have conducted the test immediately after Gilbert's electrocution.

The newspaper countered Dr. Jackson's proposal by stating that even if such an attempt proved successful, Gilbert would then have to be re-sentenced and electrocuted again.

Gilbert was buried in Cedar Grove Cemetery in Norfolk on March 21.

6

Arthelius "Felix" Christian

ARTHELIUS CHRISTIAN, a 17-year-old Black youth who was convicted in Botetourt County Court on February 18, 1909, of criminally assaulting then stabbing to death a 14-year-old White school girl, was electrocuted in the penitentiary Monday, March 22 at 7:27 a.m.

Like many more convictions to come, the "speedy justice" for Christian was predicated by "Judge Lynch." He was indicted, tried and convicted within 24 hours of his capture near Roanoke. His trial, from the time the sheriff gaveled the court to order until the sentence was pronounced, took a breathtaking 21 minutes. This was described as "the swiftest execution of justice in the history of the criminal courts of Virginia." It was all done to prevent mob violence, which according to the *Richmond Planet*, continued to be threatened up until Christian was removed to the State Penitentiary on February 20.

Christian was then executed 31 days after his conviction. Two of the witnesses to Christian's execution included the engineer and fireman of the train that carried him from Roanoke to Richmond. They had requested to witness out of curiosity, and their letter to Superintendent Morgan was penned on stationery from Richmond's exclusive Hotel Jefferson.

7

James Smith

J AMES SMITH, described by the press as a "negro tramp" 24 years of age, was found guilty of murdering James Flynn, a revered Confederate veteran. Smith was electrocuted for the crime at 7:30 a.m. on April 8, 1909.

Flynn had been in Richmond for months working odd jobs as a gardener. About midnight on January 11, he was beaten unconscious and left for dead near the Westhampton streetcar station. Some passersby, including Dr. Stuart Maclean and two streetcar employees, found him bloodied and unresponsive at about 5:40 a.m. and rushed him to the hospital, where he died without regaining consciousness. Flynn's daughters came to Richmond from Washington D.C. to claim the body.

Smith and another Black man named Charles Hamlet, who according to the *Richmond Times-Dispatch* "had bad reputations" were seen near Flynn the day of the murder, but that and all other evidence against them was purely circumstantial. Richmond's Detective Gibson had only a description of Flynn's clothing in his investigation, and when arrested, Smith was wearing a coat, trousers, and hat that supposedly matched those descriptions.

Defense Attorney A. H. Sands, who was appointed by Judge R. Carter Scott to defend Smith, intimated that before the trial was over, he would "spring some surprises in the way of evidence in favor of the prisoner." On the other hand, Commonwealth's Attorney Julienn Gunn claimed that he would "weave around Smith a fabric of facts" that would certainly send him to the electric chair.

Witness John Krug swore that he spoke to Smith at 11:40 p.m. at the Westhampton station the night before the murder. He claimed Smith acted suspiciously, telling him he was going to take the streetcar, but failed to do so when it arrived.

A critical witness for the defendant, a man named William Hill, failed to show up at the courthouse when the case was called. Judge Scott ordered the officers to find him. Later that afternoon he was found, brought to the courthouse, and fined $10 for contempt. His testimony was reported as unremarkable.

When Judge Scott sentenced Smith to death, he replied "I expected I would die for this and I do not want anyone else to die for me."

8

Berry Seaborne

BERRY SEABORNE, a "lighthearted" 22-year-old Greenville County Black man convicted of the robbery and rape of a young woman, died in the electric chair the morning of April 16, 1909. He had forced the woman at gunpoint to reveal the location of $60 that he thought she had hidden in her home. When no money was found, he allegedly shot her, although since this was a Black-on-Black crime, the details are lacking.

In 1902 Seaborne and another Black man named Jim Mason were convicted of burglary in Sussex County. He served five years in the penitentiary before he was released in 1907.

During Seaborne's confinement in Emporia, he had attempted unsuccessfully to escape but made no such attempt while held on death row in Richmond. "He remained consistently cheerful," reported the *Richmond Times-Dispatch*, "and his main object in life seemed to be to eat, and had fattened considerably after being taken to the penitentiary."

At one point Seaborne or his attorney petitioned the governor for resentencing when potentially exculpatory evidence was found. He received a short reprieve, but the *Times-Dispatch* reported "the papers contained nothing to warrant commutation."

While awaiting the execution of Seaborne, Superintendent Morgan was engulfed in letters from senior Medical College students asking if they could witness an electrocution before graduation. He responded to all that he would place their names on a list, and would contact them if a space became available.

9

John Brown

10

William Brown

JOHN BROWN and his son William, executed April 30, 1909, were two of 13 Black men arrested and charged in the February 12 murders of Mary Skipwith and Walter G. Johnson in the Skipwith home in Powhatan County. They had also robbed the house then set it on fire to cover the crime.

After looting the house, they hid some of the valuables in the stable and the outhouse. Police found the items and they supposedly contained evidence pointing to the Browns and the others. Finding similar items stashed in their homes as well, they started arresting and holding the suspects in the Farmville jail.

While in jail, the younger Brown and the two Taylors confessed details of the robbery and murders. The *Richmond Times-Dispatch* reported that "not the slightest mercy was shown the murdered man and woman, not the slightest chance for their lives was given them, but with the fiendish cruelty of starving wolves the men murdered them in cold blood."

The Browns claimed that they all arrived at "Northeast," the old Skipwith home, between 8:00 and 9:00 on the night of February 12.

Isham Taylor, who was the leader of the group, stood in front of the door with a shotgun loaded with No. 8 shot and knocked. When Walter Johnson opened the door, Taylor unloaded almost point-blank into his face.

With Johnson down, the others rushed past him into the house. When Mrs. Skipwith came into the upper hall to investigate the gunshot, one of them fatally struck her in the head with an ax. Her body was dragged to the first floor and the men began looting the house. Everything of any value was taken; even the portraits of Johnson's parents were removed and taken to the barn and outhouse. Jewelry, money, and silver were taken and divided among them.

Isham Taylor told police that while the house was being looted, Johnson regained consciousness, and with his face bleeding, begged for his life. Taylor claimed he paused looting and kicked him over on his stomach, "where he lay still." When the house was stripped almost to the bare walls, the men set fire to it in several places. Police believed Johnson was still alive when the fire was set, as his charred body was found in a spot other than where Taylor confessed he left him, indicating he may have attempted to crawl out.

Joe and Isham Taylor worked as hearse drivers, and days later, in an almost unbelievable coincidence, they drove the hearses containing their two victims to the cemetery. John and William Brown also coincidentally dug their victims' graves. John Brown became so agitated at the gravesite when he found out who the bodies were, the grave lines had to be re-drawn twice for him, raising suspicions.

Cousins Lewis Jenkins and Robert Taylor were arrested next, and while confined at Farmville they also reportedly confessed to the crime, implicating several others, including John Brown's other two sons, Emanuel and Charles Brown, William Robinson, Nannie Taylor, Ollie Ross, Stephen Johnson, and Money Johnson.

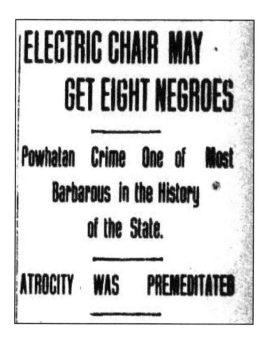

ELECTRIC CHAIR MAY GET EIGHT NEGROES

Powhatan Crime One of Most Barbarous in the History of the State.

ATROCITY WAS PREMEDITATED

Lewis Jenkins was the first to be tried. On the witness stand, he declared he was nowhere near the crime scene, but that a "divine dream" showed him all details of what had happened. He then perfectly described the entire crime, to the obvious delight of the prosecutor, and through his ill-timed "confession" a "chain of evidence was easily made against the others." While the prosecution sought the death penalty for eight of the suspects, after the trials, five of the 13 – Jenkins, Joe and Isham Taylor, and John and William Brown – were sentenced to death.

Emanuel and Charles Brown, as well as Isham Taylor's wife Nannie, were charged as lookouts and were sentenced to five years in the penitentiary. The rest were all found not guilty.

Circuit Court Judge Hundley then did something very unexpected by ordering that the five guilty men all go to the electric chair on April 30, 1909.

Hundley's decision was not well received. Governor Swanson was against five electrocutions in one day, and Penitentiary Superintendent Morgan also felt that such wholesale, assembly-line killing would make the "atmosphere of the prison decidedly depressing on the appointed day."

Yet he started making preparations. On March 27, Morgan sent a letter to Adams Electric Co., who originally wired the six-month-old electric chair, requesting extra components to have on hand for the upcoming unusually heavy load of electrocutions:

> Dear sirs; We have five subjects for the electric chair to be executed on the same day, April 30. Please quote me a price on extra helmet and leg electrode complete, and 2 extra helmet sponges. It is possible you are not familiar with all the types of negro heads and consequently, it has not occurred to you that there could be much wide departure from the normal shape; therefore if it can be done, that the helmet be made as to be flexible to some extent at least. Our last experience demonstrated the necessity for such an arrangement, as the current dried out the sponge on each side of the head ... and showered itself in sparks.

Eager to keep a customer happy, Adams replied in chilling language more suited for the seller of a household appliance, that:

> ... we will make an extra helmet of a design which will be more flexible in order to meet your special requirements in the execution of negro criminals ... We will not make any charge to you for the reason that we want you to feel perfectly satisfied in every respect and be successful with our apparatus. We also appreciate the very kind interest that you have taken in our equipment and therefore feel that it is no more than is right that we should take care of you in every detail.

Still uncomfortable with arranging five consecutive executions, Morgan called a meeting with Governor Swanson about the matter, followed up by an explanatory letter dated April 12:

> You will recall the talk I had with you several days ago in conference to the electrocution of the five men from Powhatan County. It is absolutely impossible to electrocute all of these men on the same date.
>
> I would be glad to have you respite Joe and Isham Taylor until the 5th of May and Lewis Jenkins until the 7th of May. I am afraid to undertake the execution of more than two men on the same day.

The governor took Morgan's advice. On April 30, John Brown, age 57, and his son William, age 33, were the first to be electrocuted for the Powhatan murders. John was strapped in the chair first at 7:24 a.m., and by 7:36 both he and his son were dead. Contrary to speculation that the elder Brown would finally confess, neither man said anything before their deaths.

This was the first time in penitentiary history that here were back-to-back electrocutions and the first time that a father and son had been condemned to die together.

The *Richmond Times-Dispatch* reported that by spreading the executions out over three days, the governor's actions were not showing clemency to any of the five prisoners, "but were taken in order to relieve the electric chair, as far as possible, of its odious significance, and to relieve the penitentiary officials from a duty which necessarily would greatly tax their nerves and sympathies."

It wasn't until February 2, 1951, when four Black members of the "Martinsville Seven," as well as a White man named George Hailey, were all executed in one day.

11

Joe Taylor

12

Isham Taylor

COUSINS JOE AND ISHAM TAYLOR, aged 34 and 32 respectively, convicted and sentenced to death with three others for the February 12 murder of Mary Skipwith and Walter Johnson, died in the electric chair May 5, 1909. The *Richmond Planet* reported that during the police investigation, china belonging to Skipwith was found hidden in Joe Taylor's barn under some loose tobacco leaves. They also found crockery, and a 200-pound carpenter's tool chest filled with tools and silverware.

A rumor recalling the rowdy behaviors seen at nineteenth-century hangings spread throughout Powhatan that a brass band would accompany the Taylor bodies after the execution and hold a demonstration over their graves. It did not happen.

13

Lewis Jenkins

THE LAST, and by far the most curious of the Powhatan murderers to be executed, Lewis Jenkins, the 40-year-old so-called "divine dreamer," died just after 7:00 a.m. on May 7, 1909.

The first to be tried in the murders, his own testimony convicted him when he stated on the witness stand that a dream had provided him full details of the crime, which he accurately described in his testimony.

Police also found hanging in his home a large picture of Walter Johnson, in its ornate, gilded frame.

After electrocution, Jenkins' body was taken to his family home in Powhatan, where his family and friends had prepared a burial spot within sight of where the crime occurred.

14

John Fleming

JOHN FLEMING, a 27-year-old Black native of Lunenburg County, was put to death in the electric chair on July 30, 1909, for murdering his wife. The press reported that he was convicted on testimony "that was practically undisputed."

After the murder, he fled to North Carolina but was captured near Salisbury. Governor Swanson issued an extradition order for his return on April 23.

While almost nothing is known of his life or the crime, a lot is known about his last meal. On the day of his execution, Fleming requested "haslet stew," a dish made of heart, liver, kidneys, and other organ meats. "We almost had to kill a cow to get those haslets," wrote penitentiary physician Carrington. "They were, after much trouble, gotten and prepared as requested.

John ate heartily of the stew and in a few minutes shuffled off this mortal coil."

The August 1, 1909 *Staunton Dispatch* reported that "The execution was totally devoid of spectacular incidents or sentimental features, and the grewsome [*sic*] work was conducted with the same accurate system and speed that have marked previous executions."

15

William Wise

WILLIAM WISE, a Black Petersburg man 29 years of age, was convicted and executed August 27, 1909, in Richmond for the robbery and murder of Thomas Walker, also Black. The murder occurred March 15 on a line of the Atlantic Coast Railroad, in southside Richmond.

Wise reportedly knocked Walker down with a "vicious blow" to the head, then cut his throat. He then robbed Walker while he bled to death. After the crime, Wise left Richmond for several weeks but was arrested when he ventured back.

Upon his arrest, Wise confessed to the murder, claiming that another man named Dorsey Archer forced him to cut Walker's throat. Archer was a witness before a coroner's jury on May 14, and while he had an established alibi, he did admit to being with Walker until late the night of the murder. He was subsequently acquitted.

The *Richmond Times-Dispatch* reported that the victim, Thomas Walker, "was a man of good character, and the crime has caused much feeling among the negroes."

16

Howard Bragg

HOWARD BRAGG, a 24-year-old White man convicted of murdering his brother-in-law, Thomas Drawbond, in Rockbridge County near Vesuvius, was electrocuted at 7:25 a.m. on September 24, 1909.

On the morning of March 20, someone discovered Drawbond's badly mutilated body on railroad tracks. A Detective named Funk later that day discovered a nearby hat shredded with 13 bullet holes, leading him to conclude that the previous day the victim had been shot in the back of the head and his body placed on the tracks. He also found footprints both leading to and away from the crime scene.

Bragg had a reputation as a "bad character" in Rockbridge, where he had once been convicted of petty larceny. This previous conviction, along with the fact he had gone missing just after Drawbond's body was discovered, led the detective to suspect that he had committed the murder.

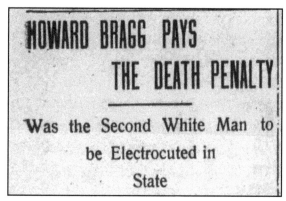

HOWARD BRAGG PAYS
THE DEATH PENALTY

Was the Second White Man to
be Electrocuted in
State

The next day, Funk heard that Bragg had applied for work at a sawmill at Irish Creek. A warrant was sworn out, but Funk and

Constable J. J. Campbell failed to find him until midnight when he was discovered asleep at the home of a fellow sawmill worker named George Tyree. When awakened, he quickly surrendered.

While at the Tyree home, Funk discovered Bragg had sold and given away several articles known to belong to Drawbond, including an Elgin watch and a Smith and Wesson revolver. Bragg tried to explain that a man named Walter Bartley committed the murder and that Bartley had given him Drawbond's possessions so he could leave the county. The detectives were not swayed, and Bragg went before a grand jury, which indicted him for murder.

During the trial in Rockbridge County Circuit Court, the court and jury were treated to "an odd spectacle" of siblings "swearing away the life of their brother with the most damaging testimony of the trial." Bragg's brother Thomas produced a magazine which he claimed his brother had given him in the jail the previous week that contained almost comically artless instructions of how to break him out. One note stated, "Tom, come around the back way some night and let me out. Come up here and get the key and let me out of jail. The key is in the kitchen on a nail."

"Don't forget to get me a saw and file," another message requested. "Get a loaf of bread and put them in it."

Two expert witnesses, W. E. McElwee and H. C. Wise took the stand to determine whether the handwriting in the magazine was similar to letters written by Howard. While noting many similarities, they ultimately testified they were unable to say for sure.

Dr. O. H. McClung, who autopsied Drawbond, testified that he was long dead from the shotgun blast to the head before the trains struck him.

As the defense tried to prove that Bragg was mentally disabled and unable to distinguish right from wrong, testimony, as well as press reports, became malevolent. One article in the *Lexington Gazette* claimed that Bragg came from a family "by no means noted for its mental caliber." Bragg's court-appointed attorney, Greenlee D. Letcher (a former House of Delegates member and son of Civil War-era Virginia Governor John Letcher), called several witnesses, including the mother of the accused, to show that a "strain of insanity" was in the young man's blood. Bragg's mother recounted her son's peculiar actions as a child, and that he frequently suffered from blinding headaches. A sister, Ninnine Bragg, committed suicide at age 17 for no apparent reason. Another brother was "weak-minded," and another was reported in the news to be "badly deformed with a head of abnormal size."

On May 19 at 4:35 p.m., W. N. Bell, foreman of the jury, rendered a verdict of guilty of first-degree murder.

In June, however, Letcher submitted a petition signed by almost all the jurors requesting clemency for Bragg. Accompanying the petition were affidavits by several individuals claiming that he "was a person of weak mind" and should not get death but life imprisonment. Bragg's July 9 execution was temporarily suspended by Governor Swanson while he reviewed the petitions.

On August 16 Letcher socialized at the Greenbrier Resort in White Sulphur Springs, West Virginia with Swanson and convinced him to continue to respite Bragg until at least September 24. In a letter to Penitentiary Superintendent Morgan, Letcher asked him to closely watch Bragg for signs of any unstable behavior that may help convince the governor to commute his sentence.

On September 21, however, Swanson decided to not interfere and allowed the execution to continue as scheduled.

On October 7, over two weeks after the execution, Bragg's mother Mary told the *Staunton Daily Leader* that the night before her son was executed, he had written a rambling confession of the murder to her, which she consented to publication on the front page of that day's edition. Among long, florid exposition that says little, Bragg claimed his attorney "was going to get me time in prison if he did not clear me and he tried to get me to play crazy but I would not do it."

17

Jack Traynham

JACK TRAYNHAM, a Black Lynchburg man, age 24, was electrocuted on November 12, 1909, at 7:00 a.m. for the murder of another Black man named Edgar Turner.

Both men worked in a livery stable, and at their lunch break got into an argument about a woman. Later that day, as they put up horses Traynham stabbed Turner several times on the left side and in the abdomen with his pocket knife. Turner died of the wounds on his way to the hospital.

At Traynham's sentencing at the Lynchburg Corporation Court on September 11, the *Richmond Times-Dispatch* reported "the negro had nothing to say."

Like every other execution since the installment of the electric chair, it reportedly "went without a hitch," and Traynham was pronounced dead just a few moments after the current was turned on.

18

Harry Baltimore

HARRY BALTIMORE, *alias* Harry Robinson, died in the electric chair December 9, 1909, for the murder of William Larkin Sealock, a White man, in Linden, just a few miles east of Front Royal.

On the day of the murder, a drunken Baltimore began making loud threats against Sealock inside a store belonging to John Hudnall. After ordered to leave the store, Baltimore staggered out to the street and fired five shots from a revolver, killing Sealock. Baltimore managed to get away in the confusion but was captured a short time later by Sheriff Marshall.

Judge T. W. Harrison in the Circuit Court of Warren County at Front Royal convicted and sentenced the 23-year-old Black man. He was the first person condemned to death in the electric chair by Judge Harrison.

19

Clifton Breckenridge

THIRTY-ONE DAYS after his trial and conviction for "attempts at criminal assault" against a six-year-old White girl, a 20-year-old "mulatto of medium height and build" named Clifton Breckenridge was executed December 17, 1909. The crime and trial took place in Staunton.

Press reports state that Breckenridge abruptly confessed the October 28 assaults to Staunton Chief of Police Liscomb, as well as to at least one fellow prisoner on November 15. A special grand jury was called the next day, November 16, at 11:00 a.m., and 45 minutes later returned an indictment. The trial began two hours later, at 2:00 p.m., and by 3:37 – after only 12 minutes of deliberation – the jury sentenced him to death.

"Never before has the town or county been the scene of a crime so damnable as to cause strong men to shudder in contemplation of its fiendish execution," shrieked a mortified *Staunton Dispatch-News*. "This crime against the sacred personage of an innocent child is too revolting to be considered dispassionately. It is a crime which cried aloud for vengeance."

Breckenridge was a Staunton jailhouse "trusty," a reliable prisoner with privileges, serving a combination of terms totaling three years for chicken stealing when the crime allegedly occurred as he cleaned the residence portion of the jail. While there, he reportedly encountered the victim, the granddaughter of the prison keeper, George Hutcheson.

The *Staunton Dispatch News* reported that "Upon finding out of the assaults, the Jailer Hutcheson took the negro in hand and administered a severe pommeling [*sic*] about the face."

For the trial, the courtroom was reportedly "jammed to capacity, with the doors and windows crowded with people." After numerous interruptions by infuriated citizens, who were demanding that Breckenridge be lynched, the prosecutor, Carter Braxton, demanded that the courtroom be cleared of everyone but the attorneys, officers, and reporters.

In his two-minute opening statement, appointed defense attorney Landes quietly affirmed that in defending Breckenridge he would "discharge the duty to the best of his ability, however unwillingly."

After inmate John Christian testified that Breckenridge had admitted his guilt to him, Breckenridge took the stand. He spoke "in a rambling disconnected way" of how he had played a game of checkers with the child, and how after the game admitted "he had committed the sacrilege with which he was charged."

After his testimony, the *Dispatch-News* stated that "The expression on the faces of the jurors was a visible indication of the fate which awaited the negro." After their fleeting deliberation, the jury foreman stood and announced "We the jury, find the accused guilty of an attempt to commit rape as charged in the indictment, and fix his punishment by death."

Despite the headline that "Prisoner Shows No Emotion," the article later observed that "With the back of his hand, the negro brushed away a single tear as he heard the verdict."

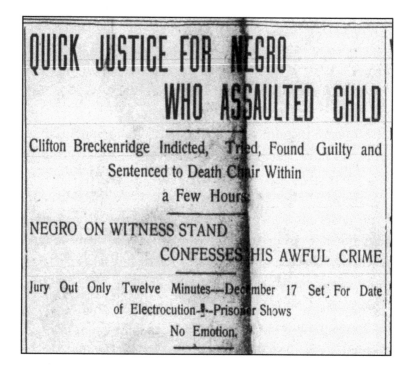

QUICK JUSTICE FOR NEGRO WHO ASSAULTED CHILD

Clifton Breckenridge Indicted, Tried, Found Guilty and Sentenced to Death Chair Within a Few Hours

NEGRO ON WITNESS STAND CONFESSES HIS AWFUL CRIME

Jury Out Only Twelve Minutes—December 17 Set For Date of Electrocution-!-Prisoner Shows No Emotion.

The next night, with anger at Breckenridge still boiling over, the Staunton fire bell sounded to summon a lynch mob. Several dozen men and boys surrounded the jail and attempted to break Breckenridge out, but they were driven back by the sheriff and several officers.

Of the breakneck conviction and sentencing, the *Dispatch-News* reported that "a blot on the fair name of the town and state has been partially obliterated and justice meted out for a crime which is horrible beyond description ... an indignity as being without parallel in the history of the state."

20

Thurman Spinner

EIGHTEEN-YEAR-OLD Black teenager Thurman Spinner was electrocuted January 14, 1910, for the murder of Charles Noell, a "well-liked" White resident of Bedford County.

Noell and Spinner were part of a larger crowd of young men who were opossum hunting the previous October when they got into an altercation, resulting in Noell tearing a small hole in Spinner's shirt, enraging him. On the way home hours later, a still riled Spinner stepped from behind a tree and struck Noell on the head with an ax. After subduing Spinner, the others carried Noell to his home, where he died three days later without regaining consciousness.

On November 4, 1909, after Noell's burial in Colfax, a mob of about 50 men traveled to the Bedford City jail with the intention of lynching Spinner. Deputy Sheriff McGhee, however, was warned of the approaching mob and took Spinner out of his cell into some nearby woods, where the two of them hid all night. The mob angrily searched the jail, then reportedly left in disgust.

21

Walter Parker

WALTER PARKER, a 25-year-old Black Norfolk resident, was electrocuted at the penitentiary on January 25, 1910.

He was convicted on December 14, 1909, of killing Sam Fisher, also Black, with a fence post. He pleaded self-defense, then made a "pathetic appeal" for a sentence of eighteen years. The meager press coverage of this case stated that the court was "visibly affected but not swayed."

22

William Goins

WILLIAM GOINS, a 38-year-old Black man from near Roanoke, was electrocuted January 28, 1910, for the June 24, 1909 shooting of Thomas Walker, described by the *Roanoke Evening News* as "a Roanoke negro of better class."

Goins had some ongoing quarrel with Walker, and one evening Goins went to Salem and saw Walker in the street. In a fit of jealous rage, he drew a pistol and shot Walker in the back, instantly killing him. Goins escaped to McDowell County, West Virginia, but was apprehended several days later.

1910

23

Howard Little

THE MOST ADRENALINE-CHARGED CRIME and trial to ever take place in Buchanan County ended November 29, 1909, when Howard Little, a petty criminal and former United States marshal of Kentucky, was found guilty of murdering six members of the Justis and Meadows family at Hurley in September. He was executed in the electric chair for the crimes on February 11, 1910.

Little was charged with ax-murdering Betty ("Aunt Betty") Justis, her son-in-law George Meadows, his wife, and their three children in late September before setting the house on fire in an attempt to conceal the killings. Married with four young children of his own, Little was having an affair with another young woman named Mary Stacy. His motivation in the murder and robbery was to steal $1,500 from Aunt Betty to leave his family while he took Miss Stacy to start a new life on the west coast.

Detective Lee Fells ordered the body of George Meadows exhumed when his investigation revealed that Little had borrowed a 32-cal. revolver from a neighbor and then returned it two days later with two chambers empty. In addition to having his head crushed with an ax, the disinterment revealed that George Meadows had also been shot twice. The bullets were located, removed, and found to be the same caliber as those from the revolver Little had borrowed.

Described by the press as "a handsome fellow of good address," Little was arrested September 25 at Bull Creek, West Virginia when Detective Fells felt that he had collected enough evidence at the murder scene to indict the McDowell County native.

On Thanksgiving morning at the Lebanon, Virginia Courthouse, jury selection took only 27 minutes, and within one hour and twenty minutes, the first witness took the stand. Betty Justis' son, Senate Justis, testified that he had worked for Little at the Ritter Lumber Company and that Little frequently asked him how much money his mother had. Another unnamed witness testified that Little told him on at least one occasion that it would be "an easy matter for someone to murder the family, rob the house then burn the victims."

Little's girlfriend, Mary Stacy, testified that Little gave her $20 the day before the murder to buy clothes for their trip west, then allegedly told her they would soon leave as he "would have plenty of money in a few days."

Mary Lee, a boarder at the Little home, described in a two-hour testimony Little's infatuation with Miss Stacy and of his troubles with his wife. She also stated Little was gone the night of the crime, and she saw him the next morning trying to file something off a lantern that she had never seen before. He then took the lantern into the woods and hid it. The lantern had belonged to Meadows, and Little was filing an identification number off of it.

Little's wife confessed in an affidavit that she had seen him the night of the murders with his clothes all bloody and torn, and he threatened that he would "kill her if she said anything to anyone about his condition." She also confessed that on the day after the murder she washed his bloody clothing.

Little never took the stand, and not a single witness was offered in his defense by his attorney, Bert Wilson.

Prosecutor Barnes Gillespie's closing arguments drew effusive press reports, describing it as "the most convincing speech ever heard in the Buchanan county courtroom." The *Newport News Daily Press* reported that:

> When [Gillespie] spoke of the horrors of that awful night in September, and how the prisoner had swept down upon that sleeping family and so cruelly butchered them and burned their bodies, the women in the courtroom sobbed aloud, while hot blood tingled in the veins of men that listened. Many eyes were filled with tears when he concluded his masterly peroration.

During the proceedings, local law enforcement reported "great difficulty" preventing Little's lynching at the hands of angry mountaineers, who were all friends of the victims.

The jury rendered a verdict of guilty in 28 minutes. Judge Burns sentenced Little to die on February 11 before he was taken from Grundy to the Roanoke jail, remaining there a short time before his transfer to the penitentiary in Richmond.

While at the penitentiary, Little informed the Rev. J. R. Johnson, pastor of Venable Street Baptist church, that years earlier he had been convicted and sentenced to life at the Kentucky penitentiary for murdering an eastern Kentucky man named George McKinney. He was pardoned after a brief imprisonment when post-trial evidence cast doubt on his guilt. However, he confessed that he did kill McKinney. Rev. Johnson also claimed Little confessed to several other crimes for which he had never been tried, but would not disclose details.

Despite his admission of guilt in the McKinney murder, Little maintained his innocence in the Justis-Meadows murders even after he walked into the death chamber at 7:00 a.m. on the fateful day. He reportedly "did not even flinch while he was strapped into the chair." Witnesses claimed he looked as if he wanted to speak, but stopped himself.

Little's body was turned over to an undertaker for preparation for shipment back to McDowell County, West Virginia.

Five minutes later, Willie Blake entered the death chamber.

24

Willie Blake

LESS THAN TEN MINUTES after the execution of notorious convicted murderer Howard Little on February 11, 1910, Willie Blake, a Black Norfolk man, was brought into the death chamber, and reportedly was dead within three minutes.

The 23-year-old Blake had been sentenced to death by the Circuit Court of Norfolk County for having attacked and injured Alice Jernigan, an elderly White woman, of Bowers Hill.

Newspaper headlines universally missed their marks with the Blake execution. "Two murderers executed," trumpeted one paper of Little and Blake, but Blake was executed for assaulting a White woman, not murder. Also, an Associated Press headline circulated that incorrectly stated Blake was "Hanged for attempted criminal assault."

25

Elijah Rouse

ELIJAH ROUSE, a 28-year-old condemned Black murderer who, along with two others, escaped from the Norfolk county jail and was later recaptured, was executed April 25, 1910.

Rouse had been tried and convicted for killing an unnamed Black man on the outskirts of Norfolk in 1909. On March 30, while jail watchman Ellsworth Huybert slept, Rouse, Thomas Noel and a so-called "powerful white Englishman" named George Nelson escaped the Portsmouth jail by cutting through the roof of the prison and lowering themselves to the ground by a rope made of torn bedclothes and pillows tied to a ventilating pipe.

The bold breakout earned coverage in newspapers all over America and even in western Canada.

Rouse and Noel separated from Nelson and stole a small rowboat to cross the Elizabeth River, but the boat sank near Lambert's Point. Both men survived but Rouse was injured on a protruding pile trying to get out of the water. The two men then made it to a friend's house in Norfolk's "Black belt" neighborhood. Alerted by a neighbor who saw the two inmates, police officers flushed the house. Rouse's injuries kept him from fleeing, and he was taken into custody.

Noel on the other hand fled as the police shot at him five times, striking him twice in the abdomen and inflicting serious injuries. He lingered near death in a Norfolk hospital before he recovered enough to be transferred to Richmond to also be executed for the murder of a Sheriff Deputy named Sykes. The *Newport News Daily Press* reported that he may have to be granted a respite "before he will be healthy enough to be executed."

Rouse was placed back in jail under 24-hour surveillance until his April 11 transfer to Richmond. George Nelson was eventually caught and received another four months tacked on to his one-year housebreaking sentence.

On April 3, the sleepy Norfolk jail watchman Ellsworth Huybert was taken into custody for permitting prisoners to escape. He faced from two to 10 years in prison.

26

Henry Smith

ON JUNE 3, 1910, while steadfastly claiming his innocence, Henry Smith died in the electric chair at 7:25 a.m. for the killing of Chicago artist and wandering vagabond Walter F. Schultz.

The Schultz murder that occurred in Alexandria, Virginia in March 1909 was a textbook case of rushes to judgment, coerced confessions, and police and prosecutorial misconduct, leading to the execution of a most likely innocent man.

On March 7, 1909, at about 10:00 a.m. a railroad worker named Richard Wines and Walter Smith, an employee of Union Station, discovered the body of an unknown White man lying in the mud in a triangular-shaped field about 100 yards east of Rosemont station, on the Washington, Alexandria and Mount Vernon electric railway, just north of the corporate limits. He was on his back, half-buried in snow, with his arms stretched at right angles. He had a ghastly wound in his neck, done by what seemed to be a jagged weapon.

The dead man was about 35 years old, 5 feet 6 inches tall, of muscular build, weighing about 160 lbs., with heavy brown hair and brown eyes. His features were prominent, with his face partially covered about two days' growth of beard.

The men hurried to Union Station and notified Baggage master L.O. Hardin, who suggested to the men and all employees that they keep away from the corpse until the police arrived on the scene to preserve any footprints that may be present there. When Alexandria Police Chief Goods and Officer Frank Simpson arrived, news of the discovery had already spread throughout the western section of Alexandria, and numerous onlookers destroyed any footprint evidence indicating the direction from which the man entered the field and whether he was accompanied by anyone else.

Upon examination, the police found inside the dead man's fashionable blue serge clothing a gold watch and a wallet containing three Wells Fargo money orders for $100 each, dated at Los Angeles on December 9, 1908, and made payable to a Walter F. Schultz. They also found $23.11 in cash, which to them ruled out robbery.

The police also found several postcards: one bore the name Alman Hume Gillette, and another was from the Berkely Apartments, at 223 North Capital Street in the District. A third card was marked "J. Burch, carriage builder."

A letter postmarked December 30, 1908, with a return address 1314 Douglas Street, Sioux City, Iowa, was addressed to Walter F. Schultz, General Delivery, Washington D.C., and published verbatim in the *Washington Times*:

> Dear Walter: You surprised us greatly when you asked us where we thought you would land next – Cuba or Chicago. We wondered whether you took a sea voyage up to Washington or went by train. We gleaned a great deal out of your descriptive letters, and enjoyed them immensely. Have you any idea where you will settle? Will you return to Chicago? Alphonse is located within nine minutes' walk of the Sears-Roebuck company store. Brother bought a suit of clothing the other day for $25. He is doing well. As ever,
>
> Ellen Dorothy

By March 8 preliminary investigations on the strange man proved his name but just deepened the mystery of his death. Alman Hume Gilette could not be located. While no carriage builder named Burch could be found, a carpenter named J.A. Burch was located, who claimed to know nothing of the dead man and insisted he gave out no business cards over the past few days. The Berkely Apartment ledger showed no one named Schultz had lived there for more than two years.

VICTIM OF ASSASSINS

WALTER F. SCHULTZ,
First Picture Published of Artist Who Was Killed Near Alexandria Early in March.

Two railway employees came forward and claimed to have seen a strange White man walking along the railroad, then lying in the field sometime later. They presumed he was drunk.

A coroner's report could not rule out murder or suicide. The horrific gash on the throat, three inches long and two inches deep, left blood only on the left side of his white collar. A prevailing theory circulated that the man might have gotten off the train at Alexandria the stormy night before the William Howard Taft inauguration and wandered in the storm into the field, where he may have been attacked. Another theory held that he had been murdered near the railway freight yards then carried to the vacant lot.

Chief Goods sent a telegram to Sioux City announcing the found body, and the next morning he received a reply from an A.H. Gillette saying "Hold body of Walter Schultz until further notice." The body was taken to Demaine and Sons Undertakers.

On March 10, Chief Goods discovered that Schultz ate lunch on Friday, the day before he was killed, at the Jackson Hotel, on King Street, an establishment populated by "a rough element." The proprietress, a woman named Jackson, and a server identified Schultz as having eaten there about 2:00 Friday afternoon. He appeared sober at lunch, according to Jackson, but witnesses who saw him board a Washington-bound train five hours later at 7:25 that night, assisted by a Black male, claimed he appeared intoxicated. The Black male was then seen by another witness boarding the rear of the same train.

The police believed that after lunch Schultz may have wandered into one of the dive bars located nearby and that he was followed by someone who saw him display his money.

City Auditor E. F. Price, T. C. Smith of the Citizens National Bank of Alexandria, and City Attorney Gardner Boothe were on the same train that carried Schultz from Alexandria to the St. Elmo station. They identified a photograph of Schultz as their fellow passenger.

"He got on the train when it turned from Cameron Street to King Street," reported Price. "He was intoxicated, and helped aboard by a negro, who then got on the rear end." Schultz and the Black male left the train at St. Elmo.

By March 13 police were no closer to solving the mystery of Walter Schultz than they were on the day his body was found. A new theory stated that Schultz was murdered in a robbery in a nearby house and carried to the vacant lot. The small amount of cash left on him was a ruse, the police believed, to support a suicide motive.

Stung by criticism of the sluggishness of the investigation, and showing much frustration, Police Chief Goods claimed he was beginning to believe the suicide theory, but he could not explain the absence of a murder weapon or the lack of blood on Schultz's clothing. Also, Walter Schultz's baggage could not be located anywhere in the District, and no one came forward to verify his accommodations.

On that day, police disputed a rumor that a local woman claimed she had given a night's lodging to a Black male the previous Saturday night for $4 and that he had to leave early Sunday morning because he claimed to have murdered a White man the night before.

Police Captain R.H. Atkinson testified at the coroner's inquest on the same day that he had seen Schultz and three other strangers on West Street about noon Saturday, between the time he was seen on the train Friday night and 9:00 a.m. Sunday morning when his body was discovered. Others who saw the quartet Saturday, and who also saw the body, testified that they did not believe Schulz was in the group. Accepting the identification of Captain Atkinson as reliable, however, some believed Schultz could have met the three men with whom he was seen with Friday night, then ridden into Alexandria with them on Saturday.

From the scarce facts in their possession, the investigators pieced together yet another theory: they believed that Walter Schultz came to Washington for the Taft inauguration, went over to Alexandria on Friday, and drank heavily before boarding an electric train. He disembarked at St. Elmo, either with or without the Black male who helped him aboard. He then spent the night with the man, or with other strangers whom he might have encountered. He came into Alexandria again on Saturday with three men. He was lured someplace and murdered in a robbery. His body was then carried to the field, where it was discovered.

On March 14 reporters discovered that a Black ex-convict named Henry Smith had been arrested but held with no charge in Alexandria, leading to speculation that he was involved with the Schultz murder. Chief Goods, however, stated that Smith was held because he had a pawn ticket for a gold watch valued at $100, bearing the name of William Thomas. Goods denied Smith was held on any other charge.

The press was baffled, however, that no one was permitted to see Smith for four days.

It was later revealed that Henry Smith was a 45-year-old Richmond native who had served two previous terms in the Virginia Penitentiary – one for stealing a diamond ring when he was fourteen years old, and another for housebreaking. While in the penitentiary he learned the upholstery trade.

Then, on March 18, Smith allegedly admitted to police that he did not kill Schultz but he did take part in the murder along with three other men – James Dorsey, Richard "Dick" Pines, and Calvin "Sonny" Johnson. Blood-stained clothing was reportedly found in all three men's possession after the identification, and they were all arrested.

Smith admitted to the Police Court that he was forced by Pines at gunpoint to participate in the murder. He testified that when he left a bar, an intoxicated Schultz had already been detained by the three outside, and they had beaten him and thrown a coat over his head as he cried: "Please don't do this to me."

They then wrestled Schultz along the railroad tracks, with Pines holding him in a headlock and Johnson carrying his feet. Once away from the city Johnson suggested they lay Schultz across the tracks and let the train kill him, but Dorsey insisted they could not get away fast enough without being seen.

Smith then claimed they carried Schultz over the hill and laid him on the ground. He thought Schultz had been smothered by the coat, as he lay still and did not say anything. Johnson and Pines then sat on his arms, holding him down, while Dorsey took a weapon of some sort and jabbed it numerous times in Schultz's neck, killing him.

After an initial hearing on March 24, the story of the murder told by Henry Smith spread and angered the people of the city. Soon a crowd filled the street by the jail, threatening a lynching and forcing the

Alexandria police to transfer Johnson, Pines, and Dorsey to the jail at Fairfax Court House. Smith remained in Alexandria.

The three prisoners were shackled together and taken under heavy guard to the train at Prince and Royal Streets. A squad of policemen reportedly "surrounded the cowering negroes," protecting them from hundreds of furious men and boys.

On April 6 a bruised and beaten Henry Smith was the principal witness at a grand jury hearing. "While the jury holds its deliberations behind closed doors," the *Washington Evening Star* reported of Smith's noticeable injuries, likely incurred in a backroom beating, "it was evident Smith had again been through a pretty severe grilling, as was evidenced by his appearance as he emerged from the jury room."

On April 22 Walter Schultz's belongings were finally located in the D.C. home of Alice Burch, wife of J. A. Burch, whose business card was found on Schultz the day his body was found. Unfortunately, Burch had committed suicide for unknown reasons only days earlier by jumping from a bridge at Second and I Streets. His wife told police that Schultz arrived in early December, and told her he was going to Baltimore after the inauguration, and that was where she believed he was when the murder occurred.

On May 23 Schultz's sister, Alman Hume Gillette, arrived in Alexandria from Iowa to testify for the prosecution in the May 25 trial of Calvin Johnson and to take her brother's belongings back to Iowa. She told a reporter that her brother was a "bit of a vagabond and a soldier of fortune," and she and their parents never really knew where he was. After Johnson, Pines went to trial June 3, then Dorsey on June 11. Smith was tried last.

Based on Henry Smith's confession, which he repeated almost verbatim at all three trials, All three were found guilty of first-degree murder and sentenced to death in the electric chair on September 3, 10, and 17, respectively.

Three times Smith claimed it was Dorsey who stabbed Schultz in the neck while the others held him down. No one offered a motive for the killing.

At sentencing, Johnson was brought in first. In a weak voice he uttered, "Well, judge, I have nothing to say except I am innocent."

Richard Pines was next ushered into the prisoner's box, where he stood and proclaimed in a clear voice "You ought to give me a show. [Henry] Smith is looking for his freedom and that is why he is keeping so quiet. I heard him tell a woman in jail about $5 and a watch, and he promised to pay her when he got out. I wish the people would give me a show so I could prove my innocence."

James Dorsey came in and also proclaimed his innocence.

Since Smith's trial was scheduled on September 24 (after two postponements), Governor Swanson signed a respite for Johnson, Pines, and Dorsey, suspending their executions until after Smith's trial. However, Smith's attorneys requested several more stays so he did not go to trial until January 5, 1910. It was expected Smith would plead guilty to second-degree murder, thus avoiding the electric chair, but for unknown reasons, Smith went to trial charged with first-degree murder. A jury had to be brought in from Charlottesville, as media attention was too intense in Alexandria to find twelve impartial jurors.

The trial lasted two days, with Smith testifying a fourth time it was Dorsey who stabbed Schultz to death. Nonetheless, on January 8, Smith was found guilty in the death of Walter Schultz.

But a few days after his conviction Smith startled even his attorneys when he confessed to Alexandria Commonwealth Attorney Crandal Mackey that he had lied under intense police coercion and that all four of them were innocent of killing Schultz. He had no thought of saving himself in making this confession, he declared, but did not wish to "face my maker until I had done all in my power to save those innocent men," who had been "brought into the shadow of death" by his false statements. Indeed, the men were mere days away from execution when Smith confessed.

Smith told Mackey that he did not know anything about Schultz's murder except what he learned from Chief Goods and Officer Sampson. His turning of state's evidence had been coached, he claimed, while he was held between March 14 and 18 in the police station and given no food or water. "The police first suggested to me that Pines and Dorsey had something to do with the murder," Smith recalled, noting how desperate the police were to solve the case. "They told me they were sure those men were guilty."

"The net was closing in on me. I decided that if I was to save myself from the chain of circumstantial evidence I had to say that Pines and Dorsey had been guilty. Later I brought Johnson into the crime to still further strengthen the story. I knew nothing about Johnson, except that he sold cocaine."

Mackey then asked Smith if the police had promised him immunity if he turned state's evidence. Smith claimed the policemen told him "You need not fear if you tell everything you know about what Pines, Dorsey, and Johnson did." Smith added that the reason he insisted on going to trial on January 5 was to tell the truth before the three others were executed since they were innocent. He also alleged that during his trial he was winked signals by Chief Goods how he should answer the prosecutor's questions.

Indignant about Smith's claim, Chief Goods branded his confession a deliberate and outrageous lie. But as a result, Governor Swanson granted yet another 60-day stay of execution for Johnson, Pines, and Dorsey.

There was of course no follow-up to Smith's admission about Goods' methods and no investigation of improper police behavior.

The confession changed nothing for Smith, as on January 14 the judge sentenced him to death in the electric chair. After the pronouncement, Smith smiled and thanked the judge. He later issued a rambling four-page statement "abounding in phonetic spelling and repetitions" that maintained, among other things, "God is satisfied with me that I have told the truth, and I didn't want to die with the crime on my mind. I ask the citizens not to take and lynch me, but let me go to the electric chair and die in a legal manner. I hope Chief Goods and Officer Sampson will prepare themselves to meet me in heaven, as they have caused me to do this wicked thing and caused me to lose my life. But God has forgiven me, and I must forgive them."

Smith was granted several respites from the chair on various legal technicalities while in the State Penitentiary, including one on March 18, 1910, when Governor Mann, it was widely believed, purposefully delayed the announcement of the stay until literally minutes before Smith was led to the death chamber, just to see if he would confess again. He did not.

As a result of the interest in the case, and the doubt thrown on all the stories due to Smith's second confession, public sentiment intensified for Calvin Johnson, Richard Pines, and James Dorsey, all still languishing on death row, having been granted six stays of execution. Petitions to commute their sentences containing over 600 signatures, including many lawyers in the D.C. area, were delivered to Governor Mann. On June 10, the governor commuted the death sentences of the three men to life imprisonment without parole.

Not one of those three men testified that Smith played a direct role in the murder of Walter Schultz. And Smith, in any of four confessions, never implicated himself. Yet he was the only one to be executed.

"People of this city, will you listen to what is true?
And I will tell you with all my heart,
What the chief made me do.
He locked me close in a cell,
Where I was bound and compelled to do just like he says,
But if I did but only refuse I should go through a terrible spell.

I wrung my hands together,
And wondered what I must do.
He then gave me a little Bible,
And told me to read,
For the lynchers may be coming after you.
Then the tears were streaming down my cheeks,
As I did holler and cry,
'Chief, let me see my wife and child once more.
Be fair, for I die, for no more liberty shall I see.
Chief, please take out your gun and kill me.'
But God is still looking and sees all over the land.
I wish he would point down his finger and show who murdered that man."

-Poem written by Henry Smith while in prison, January 14, 1910.

27

Thomas Noel

THOMAS NOEL, a condemned Norfolk county murderer, was refused a writ of error in the Supreme Court of Appeals and went to his death in the electric chair on June 10, 1910. He had originally been sentenced to die on April 25, but Governor Mann respited the sentence first to May 13, then to June 10, to allow Noel to sufficiently recover from his gunshot wounds at the hands of a sheriff's deputy to permit his execution.

Noel was executed for his August 28, 1909 murder of Joseph W. Sykes, a deputy sheriff of Norfolk County. He was sentenced to death on February 17. As reported earlier, on March 30 he, with two other prisoners named George Nelson and Elijah Rouse, escaped from the

Norfolk jail then recaptured after a widely-reported chase. Noel was captured April 6 at Drummond's Woods on the outskirts of Norfolk after a continuous 24-hour pursuit with bloodhounds. Before being taken, he took two loads of buckshot to the stomach from a policeman, seriously wounding him.

There was considerable confusion as to the correct identification of Noel as the murderer of Deputy Sheriff Sykes. Sykes and another officer were attempting to arrest Noel and two others when one of them shot him. This arrest occurred at night, so the defense's main argument was to prove that the identification of Noel by the other officer was insufficient.

An eye-opening phrase in the 110-year-old writ of error in his shooting reverberates today, which states "That officers are far too frequently hasty in taking the life of negro prisoners is only too well known."

28

Angelo Hamilton

AFTER THREE TRIALS and six gubernatorial respites, 27-year-old Angelo S. Hamilton, a White North Carolina native and murderer of Sallie Hix, was electrocuted at 7:00 a.m. on July 1, 1910.

The crime occurred at Knitting Mill Hill in South Lynchburg on the night of June 1, 1909. Obsessed with Hix, an intoxicated Hamilton saw her at a public picnic that he had ordered her not to attend. When she refused to leave, or allow him to accompany her, he shot her twice, with one of the bullets severing her spinal column. She died soon afterward.

His defense was that the shooting was accidental. A witness to the shooting, John Armstrong, claimed also that the shooting was not intentional, but that the intoxicated Hamilton was recklessly waving his pistol when it accidentally discharged.

Governor Mann reviewed the defense but refused to intervene, declaring that the evidence was insufficient and that Armstrong's testimony that the shooting was accidental was not only unconvincing but improbable.

Hamilton's sister, a Mrs. Lane of Durham, North Carolina along with numerous friends also petitioned Governor Mann for executive clemency, to no avail. A final respite was granted one week before execution so that Hamilton's wife and children could visit from Oxford, North Carolina.

Hamilton, who was described by the press as leading "a life of degeneracy" before his arrest, embraced religion and spent the last weeks of his life reading his Bible, appearing reconciled to his fate. He went to the chair without a sound and made no final statement. His body was taken to North Carolina for burial.

29

Arch Brown

MIDDLEBROOK RESIDENT ARCH BROWN was a mean drunk, and on September 22, 1910, it got him the electric chair.

Brown was 32 years old, but very little else is known of him, other than he was considered "a good hand." Brown often worked together with two friends, Abe Hoy and Abe's older brother Perry at sawmills, farms, and other similar jobs around southern Augusta County.

On May 8, Brown, Abe Hoy, and several others were playing cards at the home of J.W. Ross, a tenant on the Middlebrook farm of John

Irvine, where Brown was employed at the time. Brown and Hoy had been drinking cheap whiskey for two straight days, and when Hoy won all of Brown's money he drunkenly taunted him.

Angered by his friend's taunts, an equally inebriated Brown went to the Irvine's and borrowed a repeating pump shotgun and several cartridges under the pretense of shooting a sheep-killing dog. He returned to the Ross house but found himself locked out.

Brown loaded the gun, then paced back and forth, shouting "Come out or I'll kill you in there!" Abe Hoy's brother Perry came out of the house with his hands up in an attempt to calm the furious Brown, but when Brown raised his gun at him he jumped over a picket fence and took off running. Suddenly a shot roared through Perry's hat, grazing his scalp and knocking him down. Terrified, Perry tried to scramble to his feet but Brown shot him again, in the back. Perry stumbled another few steps, then fell dead.

Noticing movement inside the house, Brown blindly shot several times, killing a 6-year-old boy named Cletis Higgs and wounding the boy's father, Edwin Higgs, both who were visiting Abe Hoy.

In a panic, Abe Hoy ran out the back door attempting to escape to Irvine's house. Brown saw his friend and fired repeatedly, striking him four times, but Hoy managed to keep running. Brown then walked to Irvine's, thinking that was where Hoy was going but was unable to find him.

John Irvine calmed the anxious, reeling Brown, then convinced him he needed to go into Staunton and turn himself in. Brown agreed, and Irvine carried him in a buckboard to the city jail. Once there, Brown expressed regret to the jailer for killing Perry Hoy and Cletis Higgs but was sorry he did not kill Abe Hoy, who got all his money.

After several delays, the trial began July 14, and Brown was found guilty of first-degree murder. Brown's attorney Blease moved that a new trial be ordered to allow more time to gather all evidence, but the motion was denied.

Brown was ordered to stand. The judge expounded on the heinous-ness of his crime, the fairness of his trial, and the able manner in which he had been defended, then proceeded to sentence him to be electro-cuted on September 22. Brown received his sentence calmly, with no expression.

On September 9, two officers arrived from the penitentiary to es-cort Brown and another prisoner, Pink Barbour of Rockingham County, to their executions. The two were shackled together to thwart any escape attempts.

The *Staunton Dispatch* reported that "While Brown remained stoic and expressed no regret of his actions during his trial when chained to Barbour, however, he finally seemed to realize the depths to which he had sunk. He was reportedly sobbing when he boarded the train."

30

Pink Barbour

A BLACK AUGUSTA COUNTY MAN, Pink Barbour, age 22, was put to death on September 23, 1910, for the July 4 murder of James Lee in Harrisonburg. Barbour was accused of shooting Lee outside a stable where Lee was employed after Barbour refused to leave the store.

But suspiciously altered court transcripts show Barbour's trial was a fraud, with Barbour erroneously convicted, then wrongfully exe-cuted, possibly at the whim of a judge.

Witness testimony stated that Lee had seen Barbour standing near some whips in his store. Lee asked what he was doing and Barbour re-plied he was just looking at them. Lee then told him to leave, which he did "in a hesitating manner." Lee's employer, W.D. Garber, then also ordered him out of the store or he would call the police. Barbour moved very slowly, and Lee told him as he picked up a pine board that he would "paddle him out."

Barbour then went away to Water Street and Lee threw down the board. Barbour returned, however, and reportedly told Lee, "I'll get even with you." When Lee picked up the plank again, Garber claimed Lee had followed Barbour out and around the corner.

Garber testified did not see the shooting but heard three reports and saw Barbour running away. Another witness, Flint Gassway, saw Lee with his hand raised, with the board in it about to strike Barbour, and he was in that position when he was shot. He asserted that Lee had been talking abusively to Barbour.

Charles A. Johnson was the very first man to seize Barbour after the shooting. He claimed he saw him coming from the stable with Lee after him. He also maintained Lee had no stick, but that Barbour turned while Lee was standing still and fired three shots in quick succession. He did not think Barbour was intoxicated.

T. S. Sandy, who also subdued Barbour after the shooting, understood him to say, "I'll shoot you if you don't turn me loose."

Jacob Lamb, a policeman who helped to arrest Barbour, claimed he had been drinking. Forty-five minutes after Barbour was put in jail, Lamb testified the prisoner fell into a drunken stupor.

Barbour took the stand and stated that he could not remember shooting Lee. He recalled that he had several drinks with some Grottoes friends, but that he was not in the habit of getting drunk, and had not been drunk since last winter.

Barbour's level of inebriation was key to the testimony. In the first instruction to the jury, Judge Haas stated "When a homicide has been committed by a person in such a condition of drunkenness as to render him incapable of a willful, deliberate and premeditated purpose, the jury cannot find the prisoner guilty of murder in the first degree," and thus not eligible for the electric chair.

A parade of witnesses testified that Barbour was extremely intoxicated at the time of the crime. Dr. Frank Miller, who saw him on the street before the shooting, testified that Barbour was too drunk to pick up some change he had dropped.

On July 22, the arguments concluded and Judge Haas retired the jury to deliberate. After only 15 minutes they unanimously found Barbour guilty of first-degree murder.

Something disturbing had happened. The typed transcript of the trial records shows Miller testifying "that Barbour at that time [of the murder] was drunk." That line, however, was crossed out in pencil and changed to "appeared to be under the influence of drink, that is to say very jolly and talkative."

Another typed line stating "That Lee had the stick up raised as though to strike and moved quickly towards Barbour" was also hand-altered to "... Lee did not get within striking distance of Barbour within sight of the witness."

Those changes, most likely by Judge Haas, as only he had access to the transcripts, eradicated any claims of self-defense and also charged that Barbour was not drunk, in defiance of the witness's testimonies. These changes made Barbour eligible for the death penalty instead of the more appropriate 25 years in the penitentiary.

Counsel's request to grant a new trial because "the verdict ... was contrary to the law and the evidence ..." was unfortunately overruled. "The public generally, it is understood, approved the verdict and believe that Pink Barbour was given a fair and impartial trial," reported the July 29, 1910, *Staunton Spectator*.

On September 9 two officers came from Richmond to escort Barbour to the State Penitentiary death row. He was executed at 7:27 a.m.

31

John Eccles

JOHN ECCLES went to his death in the electric chair on November 11, 1910, for stabbing to death Sidney Woods, another Black man, on a train returning to Roanoke from Winston-Salem. Eccles confessed that he and four others – James Hairston, Will Cowan, Piggie Pen, and Thomas Bailey – were drinking heavily on the train when a quarrel broke out, but that all the other men were innocent except himself and another, Walter Joyce, who was never caught.

Press reports stated that the killing occurred in March in Henry County, "with a free fight beginning when the negroes were 'charged up' with liquor. Eccles claimed he was trying to protect himself when Woods was killed." All four men – Eccles, Cowan, Hairston, and Bailey – were originally sentenced to death.

On July 22, attorney D. D. Hawkins tried to secure a pardon for three of the men. Some of the petitioners suggested a pardon, others a short penitentiary sentence, while E.J. Davis, foreman of the grand jury, asked the governor to commute the sentences of all the men to life imprisonment without parole. Seventeen-year-old Eccles triggered the clemency requests after he insisted that only he and Joyce were responsible for the killing, but that Joyce struck the fatal blow.

On August 7 a respite was granted until November 11 to await the trial of Piggie Pen. Pen had escaped to Winston-Salem just after the murder but had been recaptured and returned to Danville, where he awaited trial. His trial results are unknown, although he was not put to death.

All of the men testified that Joyce was the actual murderer. Eccles, however, was still executed.

On December 31, the death sentences of Hairston and Bailey were commuted to life imprisonment, and Cowan received 18 years in the penitentiary.

32

Waverly Coles

NEWPORT NEWS CHIEF OF POLICE MITCHELL traveled to Richmond on November 26, 1910, to attend by special invitation of the superintendent of the State Penitentiary the execution of 20-year-old Waverly Coles.

Coles, a Black man originally from North Carolina, shot Edward Fenner twice around 6:00 p.m. the evening of August 20, "with one bullet entering his breast and the other his side, splitting his liver," according to the *Richmond Planet*. The shooting occurred in the Manchester part of Richmond.

Fenner did not die right away, and when police located him badly injured in the tan-yard bottom, he told them Coles shot him. He was taken to a doctor, but he died later of his injuries. Coles told police that he shot Fenner because he owed him a dollar, which he would not pay back.

While treating Fenner, doctors found a chunk of china plate stuck in his skull. Fenner gasped out that earlier that day he argued with a woman named Martha Williams, who had hit him over the head with several plates, with one piece striking him so hard it became embedded.

Williams was arrested and later tried for felonious assault.

A jury made up of 11 White men and one Black man deliberated Coles' fate for 37 minutes but was deadlocked on the first ballot, with seven voting for the death penalty and five for second-degree murder, which called for a sentence of 18 years. On the second deliberation, all 11 Whites voted for death, with the Black man the lone holdout. The third ballot reached a unanimous verdict when the Black jurist finally voted for death.

Chief Mitchell had the distinction of being the first Newport News resident to see a criminal executed in Virginia's electric chair. He told the *Newport News Daily Press* that he did not care to see anymore, "as the sight was very horrifying."

The *Richmond Times-Dispatch* reported, as was customary boiler-plate for Black-on-Black crimes, that "Public opinion seemed to agree that Coles' sentence was just, that he had an impartial trial, and that according to the evidence no other sentence could be carried out."

33

John J. Smyth

THERE WAS A DOUBLE EXECUTION on December 16, 1910, when John Smyth, a 34-year-old White bartender from Norfolk, and Harry Sitlington, a Black farm hand, age 17, both went to the chair within minutes of each other for murder.

Smyth, who went to the chair first, was convicted of shooting his wife, Bridget Smyth, and young daughter, Rita Mae on August 31 while severely intoxicated. Notorious among his family as an abusing alcoholic, Smyth had allegedly on several occasions drunkenly threatened Bridget's life.

On the morning of the murders, Smyth had "about sixteen drinks" before he returned home, drew a revolver and fired four shots, with two striking his wife and one striking his daughter as she tried to shield her mother. Two other young daughters and a son in another part of the house escaped injury.

On September 15 the Norfolk Police placed Smyth's son, eight-year-old William, under the charge of the police matron after information reached them that the young boy may be kidnapped by family members to prevent him from testifying against his father.

At the trial, the younger Smyth was a material witness and testified to the alcoholism of his father and the resulting frequent quarrels between his parents. Despite the elder Smyth's defense of alcoholic insanity, he was found guilty and sentenced to the electric chair.

On November 10, defense attorney Alfred P. Thom argued for a new trial, asserting that the jury in its verdict had been unduly influenced by Commonwealth Attorney Tilten's statement that an "improper relationship" between Smyth and his wife's sister from Boston was the motive behind the shooting, but that no substantiating evidence was presented. Also, Thom argued that Smyth's son, the principal witness for the prosecution, had been coached while in police custody to testify against his father. The court refused both arguments.

On November 21, when Smyth left Norfolk for Richmond to await execution, a crowd estimated 500 strong gathered around the jail to watch as Smyth's three children were brought from St. Mary's Catholic Orphanage to say goodbye to their father. As Smyth knelt and kissed all three children, many women reportedly "screamed in anguish," with one fainting at the heartbreaking sight of Smyth with his children. Several others reportedly "ran weeping from the scene."

Smyth's last words to the Norfolk police captain were "Find a home for my children, Captain, and take good care of that boy. Tell all goodby for me."

On November 27, attorney Thom appealed to Governor Mann to commute Smyth's sentence to life in prison, then again on December 18, to no avail.

34

Harry Sitlington

SEVENTEEN-YEAR-OLD HARRY SITLINGTON died in the electric chair within minutes of John J. Smyth on December 16, 1910.

Sitlington was only 16 when he was convicted in October of murdering 55-year-old Fannie Brown with a club near Walker's Creek in Rockingham County. He admitted the killing but also implicated two local White boys in the murder.

On October 22, Robert Brown, who owned the property and lived there with his elderly mother and his sister Fannie, left home on business. According to press reports, Harry and his mother, Amy Sitlington also had lived with the Brown's for about four years as helpers. Before leaving, Robert told Harry to clean out a ditch in their orchard.

Shortly after lunch, Fannie, while on her way into the barn to gather eggs, saw the teen near the barn "idling his time." She admonished him to get back to work, but "The boy told her he did not like having two bosses and exhibited an ugly temper." She then entered the barn.

An hour or so later Harry's mother went into the barn and found Fannie Brown lying on the floor seemingly dead, with severe bruises on her head and face. She ran back to the house and reported the incident to Fannie's mother, who assumed maybe her daughter had fallen from the loft. They called a neighbor, and after a quick examination, claimed the woman appeared to have been murdered.

More neighbors rushed over, as did Drs. Morrison of Rockbridge Baths, and Martin of Brownsburg. Justice D. L. Ward and Constable A. L. White arrived shortly afterward.

During questioning by Ward and White, Sitlington confessed that he assisted in the murder with two local White boys named Stuart and Clarence Jarvis. He described how the three of them had planned and committed the murder because of the Jarvis boys' hatred of the Browns. He also claimed the brothers had forced him to assist under a threat of violence.

He later confessed to Justice Ward, however, that the two Jarvis boys had nothing to do with the murder.

Sitlington was a small boy, barely five feet in height and not more than 100 pounds. He was dwarfed by his penitentiary-issued shirt. The press reported that "the boy had a criminal look and seemed not to realize the enormity of his crime. He expressed sorrow for the deed, but it seemed the sorrow of fearing punishment rather than remorse for his crime."

As usual, the press reported that the executions of Sitlington and Smyth went without a hitch. "Both men were calm and stoic in the face of death, and neither had anything to say."

1911

35

Richard Biggs

RICHARD HARDING BIGGS, a Black 28-year-old Raleigh, North Carolina man, went to the electric chair on January 7, 1911, after being convicted in Newport News of murdering his one-time live-in girlfriend, Annie Davis, described only as "a young mulatto woman."

Biggs and Davis lived together for at least a year in Raleigh but after enduring ongoing physical abuse Annie returned home to her mother in Virginia. Biggs traveled to Virginia and confronted her several times about returning, but she refused to have anything to do with him.

On June 11, 1910, "after taking several drinks," Biggs approached her on Jefferson Avenue in Newport News. She replied she did not care to talk to him and walked away. As she turned Biggs pulled a revolver from his coat and fired four times, with three shots striking her. He stood quietly as an angry crowd surrounded him, but then was apprehended and taken to the city jail.

The funeral of Annie Davis was held June 14 and was "well-attended by the Black community." They also reportedly expressed disgust for Biggs, as they considered Davis a friend and viewed her murder as a senseless, cold-blooded act.

On June 15 the police were swamped by inquiries about Biggs when a rumor spread that he died of fright inside his cell. Not knowing how or why the rumor originated, they nonetheless put Biggs under 24-hour suicide watch.

Biggs admitted at trial that the reason he made no effort to get away after the shooting was that the crowd of Blacks who quickly assembled before police arrived was exceptionally hostile, and he feared they would attack him if he tried to run. An arresting officer claimed Biggs pleaded with him to not let the crowd hurt him.

On September 20, Biggs "heard his death sentence without flinching," then was taken to the Newport News jail. On December 8, a fellow prisoner named Esau Johnson conducted a religious service for the repose of Biggs' soul before he left for Richmond.

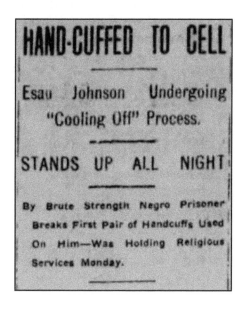

HAND-CUFFED TO CELL

Esau Johnson Undergoing "Cooling Off" Process.

STANDS UP ALL NIGHT

By Brute Strength Negro Prisoner Breaks First Pair of Handcuffs Used On Him—Was Holding Religious Services Monday.

On a side note, Esau Johnson was a Christian man but also was described in the Newport News press as "the meanest prisoner ever incarcerated" at the city jail. He initiated uprisings, beat other prisoners, and threw pots of beans, water, and anything else he could get his hands on. At one point he had to be handcuffed to his cell bars but with pure brute strength broke away. After finding no volunteers to go inside Johnson's cell, Jailer Wiley went in with his gun drawn and double-shackled Johnson's hands and feet again to the bars, where he remained standing upright all night in a "cooling off" period.

On December 23, 1910, the Supreme Court of Virginia and the governor denied a final commutation request, and Biggs was sent to the State Penitentiary to die.

36

Alex Holloman

ON JUNE 2, 1911, 24-year-old Alex Holloman, a Black Virginia Beach native, was executed at 7:28 a.m. for the murder of his wife, Martha Holloman (and possibly a child, records are unclear). The murder occurred on February 23, 1911, in Princess Anne County, when Holloman, believing his wife had been unfaithful, "with malice aforethought" shot her in the chest and abdomen, killing her.

Holloman's attorney moved to continue the March 27 trial since he had not enough time to prepare a competent defense, but the motion was overruled. The attorney then moved that a special jury be empaneled to inquire into the sanity of the defendant, but the court overruled that motion also, stating that there was no evidence to show Holloman was "of unsound mind."

Originally scheduled to be executed on May 12, Holloman received one respite to June 2.

37

Henry Clay Beattie Jr

"Here comes Henry Clay Beattie in an automobile,
He's running so fast that you can't see the wheel;
With a ring on his finger and a gun in his hand,
He's trying to put the murder on an innocent man."

-Virginia folk song, c. 1912, composer unknown

WHITE CAPITAL DEFENDANTS who are wealthy enough to afford their own attorneys almost universally do not get put to death. Henry Clay Beattie Jr. was an exception.

Beattie, of 1529 Porter Street in Richmond, went to his death in the electric chair on November 24, 1911, for the July 18 murder of his wife, Louise Wellford Owen Beattie. Beattie's case was described in a hastily-published 1912 book called "The Great Beattie Murder Case" as "truly a pathetic picture of twentieth-century civilization, a sad commentary on the wild passions of the day, and a pitiable condition of human affairs which once more verified the biblical pronouncement that 'the wages of sin is death.'"

Born September 28, 1884, Henry was one of five children of Mattie Fowler Belote Beattie and Henry Clay Beattie Sr., a wealthy businessman. He had received a good education but lived a spoiled, reckless life of irresponsibility.

In 1907, the 23-year-old Henry started dating a 13-year-old girl named Beulah Binford, who "had a reputation for being fast." Two years later she gave birth out of wedlock and gave the child up to Mary Trout of Roanoke. The little boy, named Henry C. Beattie Trout, died at age 11 months of infant cholera and was buried in Shockoe Hill Cemetery.

Never admitting paternity, and still planning to marry Louise, Beattie convinced Binford to move to Raleigh, North Carolina, and made her promise to remain there.

Beattie's marriage to Louise, a native of Dover, Delaware, pleased his father, whom the younger Beattie depended on for support. The marriage was not a happy one, yet they had a son, named Henry Clay Beattie III.

Beattie continued to cheat on his wife, and by coincidence ran into Binford at a baseball game in Norfolk. Falling for her all over again, he subsequently asked her to move to Richmond and promised to buy her a house there.

Beattie and Beulah then met secretly at various hotels and resorts around the city. His father later learned of the affair, however, and threatened to withdraw support of his son, placing Henry in a difficult situation.

In July 1911, Louise Beattie and the baby went to visit for several days an uncle, Thomas E. Owen, in South Richmond. On the 18th, Henry picked her up in his automobile for a "pleasure ride." Then, at 11:00 p.m. that night he returned to Owens' home, driving with one hand, with the other cradling his bloody and lifeless wife. Beattie claimed to Owen that they had been confronted along Midlothian Turnpike near a railroad crossing by a tall man with a long beard, who had stepped out into the road and forced the car to a stop.

Beattie claimed the stranger told him "You had better run over me," and that he replied, "You have got all the road," and tried to go around him. At that point, he claimed the bearded man raised his gun and fired. The shot entered Louise Beattie's face, allegedly blowing off the top of her head.

Beattie asserted he jumped from the car and wrestled with the stranger, and while they were struggling the unknown man raised the gun and struck him across the face. The stranger, according to Beattie, then dropped the gun, broke loose, and made off through the woods. Beattie threw the gun in the back of his automobile and rushed back to his car, and holding his dead wife beside him, raced to Owens' house. He claimed that the gun fell out of the car along the way.

Early the next morning Detective Scherer, Deputy Sheriff Sydnor, along with two caretakers from the penitentiary and two bloodhounds searched along Midlothian Turnpike for any trace of the bearded man. The bloodhounds merely ran in circles, not able to pick up any scent. The men were later joined by several more Richmond deputies, who also found it strange that no scent could be found.

While they searched, word reached them that a local Black woman named Mandy Alexander had found a shotgun with a no. 6 shell still in it lying on the Belt Line Railroad track, about 25 feet from the road, near the very spot where Beattie claimed the shooting took place.

It dawned on the police that there had been no tall man with a beard at all, but that Henry Beattie himself, telling lie after lie, pulled the trigger on his wife inside the car, then threw the shotgun out onto the tracks. They returned to Owens' home and asked Beattie to return to where the shooting had occurred, which he did. Displaying remarkable calmness, Beattie coolly answered all the detective's questions, refuting such queries as the strange angle the shooting had occurred, how far the gun was from his wife's face, and how the gun got out on the tracks. He answered slowly and concisely, and carefully considered each question before replying.

He then asked Detective Scherer if the bloodhounds had picked up a scent. "Mr. Scherer looked Beattie square in the eye and said there was no trail to be found," reported the *Richmond Times-Dispatch*. "Beattie only returned the stare of the detective, and did not for an instant lose control of himself."

A large number of people attended Louise Beattie's July 20 funeral, where Henry finally displayed some emotion, seeming "somewhat grieved." At the coroner's inquest on July 22, Beattie took the witness stand for three and a half hours for a grueling cross-examination. He never flinched, and though wide discrepancies were pointed out in his story, he never backed down. In the afternoon after lunch he was again on the stand, and many of the secrets of his life, including his affair with Beulah Binford, were revealed. Against the advice of his counsel, he refused to answer most questions about this affair.

Late in the afternoon Binford, the "other woman in the case," took the stand and directly contradicted much of Beattie's testimony, relating in sordid detail her relations with the accused before and since his marriage, including their trips to a "questionable resort" at midnight the day before the crime. A letter from Beattie to her, sending "oceans of kisses," and enclosing $10 for payment for furniture for her house, was entered into evidence.

The day before the inquest, on July 21, Beattie's cousin Paul D. Beattie, at the urging of his grandmother, Elizabeth Black, was rumored to be talking to police about the shotgun used in the killing. During the inquest lunch break on the 22nd, the case against Henry Beattie blew open when Paul, after throwing a fit of temporary insanity at his home and having to be transferred to a hospital, signed an affidavit that stated the following:

> I, Paul D. Beattie, hereby state that during the week of July 10 Henry C. Beattie called me up at my house and asked me to meet him at the corner of Short and Main Streets, which I did, and after meeting him we talked for a while, and he asked me to buy him a shotgun, whereupon I asked him what he wanted it for, and he didn't tell me what he wanted it for. I told him that I would, whereupon I went to a pawn-shop in Sixth Street and priced a single-barreled shotgun, the kind he had advised me to get, and on the following

Saturday night, about 10:15 o'clock, which was July 15, 1911, in company with Henry C. Beattie, in his, the said Henry C. Beattie's, automobile. I went to the pawnshop and secured the gun, paying $2.50, and delivering the gun to Henry C. Beattie, whereupon we both got into the automobile, and he, the said Henry C. Beattie, brought me home, arriving at home about 11:15 P. M. July 15. I also state that I bought three shotgun shells from W. B. Kidd's hardware store, at the corner of Harrison and Cary Streets, on the afternoon of July 15, 1911, and gave them to Henry C. Beattie.

(Signed)

P. D. Beattie.

The investigation concluded that Louise Owen Beattie had indeed been killed by her husband, Henry Clay Beattie, Jr. He was arrested at the end of the inquest and placed in the Henrico County Jail, where he seemed content to smoke cigarettes and strum his guitar. Paul Beattie and Beulah Binford were also arrested as accomplices.

Several Black men who had been arrested on suspicion were released from jail.

Richmond's social circles were in an uproar as the story for days dominated the front page of the *Richmond Times-Dispatch*. On August 6, while awaiting trial, a stoic Beattie posed in his jail cell for Richmond photographers Homeler & Clark. "For ten minutes he remained under the eye of a camera, and no artist ever found a subject so much at ease, so quiet, so still," reported the press.

"These people who think they are going to put me in the electric chair are all wrong," a defiant Beattie told a reporter in early August. "I shall never be electrocuted. I'd take poison and kill myself in order to prevent anything like that."

The trial began August 14, and the State produced a parade of witnesses to contradict Beattie's account of a bearded stranger killing his wife. Paul Beattie's affidavit also proved to the jury that Henry Beattie was without a reasonable doubt the man who had killed his wife. The shotgun purchased by Beattie at the pawnshop was proven to be the one used in the killing.

Henry was found guilty of first-degree murder. Judge Watson passed a sentence of death on him, closing with the ominous words "Friday, November 24th, between sunrise and sunset, your life is to be taken in the manner prescribed by law. May God have mercy upon your soul."

He did not seek an appeal.

On November 14, Paul Beattie threw a wrench into the sentence and put himself in danger of perjury when he swore another affidavit, this time claiming that he lied about buying the shotgun. "I would give anything if I had not done it," he stated of his previous admission. The new admission was not entered.

Also, on that same day Henry Clay Beattie Sr., the father of the prisoner, appealed personally to Governor Mann to commute his son's sentence to life imprisonment. A final and equally fruitless appeal to the governor was made by defense attorneys H.M. Smith and Hill Carter.

Beattie walked quietly to the death chamber on the morning of November 24. His spiritual advisors, Reverends J. J. Fix, and Benjamin Dennis were with him and administered to him the Holy Sacrament of extreme unction (last rites).

After his electrocution, he was buried beside the wife he so brutally and heartlessly murdered in a family plot in Maury Cemetery in Richmond. Their shared headstone reads "Beyond the River."

After the execution, a confession made by Beattie in the presence of the two ministers was made public:

> I, Henry Clay Beattie, Jr., desirous of standing right before God and man, do on this, the 23d day of November, 1911, confess my guilt of the crime charged against me. Much that was published concerning the details was not true, but the awful fact, without the harrowing circumstances, remains. For this action I am truly sorry, and believing that I am at peace with God and am soon to pass into His presence, this statement is made.
>
> (Signed) Henry Clay Beattie, Jr.
> Rev. J. J. Fix.
> Rev. Benj. Dennis.

While the anonymous song about Beattie at the top of this chapter circulated at the time of his execution, on March 22, 1927, the Victor Talking Machine Company released a ballad by Virginia performer Kelly Harrell, titled "Henry Clay Beattie," with the tune based on the Welling and McGhee hymn "Knocking at the Door:"

Friday as the sun was lifting,

After the sun shown clear;
Down in a cell set a prisoner,
Trembling with mercy and fear.

In came his grey-headed father,
Says, "Henry this day you must die,
If (you) don't confess that you killed her,
You'll go to your doom with a lie."

In came his brother and sister,
To bid him their last farewell;
"If (you) don't confess that you killed her,
You'll spend eternity in hell."

"Yes, I confess that I killed her,
I've taken her sweet life away;
But oh, how greedy and brutish,
I was for taking her sweet life."

'Twas late on Thursday evening,
After the sun went down;
Henry Clay Beattie was saying
Farewell to his friend native town.

Then Friday, as the sun was rising,
Just before the sun shown clear;
Henry Clay Beattie was dying,
In a 'lectric chair.

1912

38

John Williamson

I N STARK CONTRAST to the frantic, weeks-long front-page coverage of Henry Clay Beattie Jr., the press coverage of the March 15, 1912 electrocution of a 30-year-old Black laborer John Williamson was relegated to meager sentences in back pages.

Williamson went to the electric chair for the November 30, 1911 murder of his Black supervisor, Ellis Watkins, at South Boston, where both were employed in the stemmery of the Imperial Tobacco Company. Watkins had worked for many years at the company and was a well-liked foreman. Williamson had only been employed for two weeks after arriving from Danville.

Watkins approached Williamson about some substandard work, which he took as a personal insult. Williamson allegedly drew a pistol from his coveralls and shot Watkins, killing him instantly.

Williamson fled Imperial but was captured that same night by Officer Hubert Moorefield on South Boston's Upper Main Street. He received one respite from the governor in January 1912 at the request of the Halifax County commonwealth's attorney when according to the press "additional evidence having been discovered since the conviction of the negro."

The discovery, whatever it was, was not enough to save his life.

39

William Price

40

John Furby

WILLIAM PRICE and John Furby, two 20-year-old Black inmates on a Chesterfield County road crew, were executed within twelve minutes of each other on June 14, 1912, for an attack on their guard Thomas Belcher, leaving him in a critical condition that resulted a day later in his death. Price went to the chair at 7:18 a.m. and Furby at 7:30 a.m.

The attack on Belcher was considered by the Richmond press as "one of the most deliberate that has ever occurred in Chesterfield County." The "negro jailbirds" under Belcher's supervision were repairing a section of road near Ettrick, with the work requiring a pick-ax. Claiming that the ax handle was loose, one of the men borrowed a guard's knife to fix it. The knife was then passed over to either Furby or Price, and while Belcher's back was turned he was stabbed. As he turned back to defend himself, one of the men struck him on the back of his head with the blunt side of the ax.

Seriously injured, Belcher continued to single-handedly fight back, seriously wounding a third convict, William Smith, who got away but was later caught by a posse near Farmville. He died in the hospital from his injuries.

The attack occurred so quickly that most of the other crew members did not even realize what had happened until the three men had escaped. Belcher was taken to Petersburg hospital, where he died without regaining consciousness.

A Chesterfield grand jury returned against Price and Furby a charge of murderous assault and highway robbery against a law enforcement officer. Both were sentenced to death by Judge Southall on April 5.

41

Clarence Nixon

CLARENCE NIXON "went through the door" as the press reported and died in the electric chair on June 21, 1912, for the "despicable crime" of rape.

The case of 24-year-old Nixon, a Black resident of Norfolk County, is complicated, as the *Alexandria Gazette* describes a completely different crime as the *Richmond Times-Dispatch* and the *Mathews Journal*, the only Virginia papers to cover the offense.

According to the Alexandria paper, 35-year-old Mrs. William Stiles awakened in her home on the Dismal Swamp Canal near Portsmouth to "a negro who was in her apartment." She screamed and began fighting, attracting her mother to the bedroom, "and the two scratched and tore at him and screamed for assistance" until he fled. He was caught by neighbors soon after, and the paper stated that "unless he can prove a better alibi than the one he has already given to the police, it is said he is likely to go to the electric chair."

According to the account in the *Journal* and the *Times-Dispatch*, the victim was a White married woman who was allegedly called out of her house around midnight by Nixon under the pretext that her husband, a boatman, had asked her to come to the river.

Once out in the yard Nixon allegedly attacked the woman, subjecting her to "horrible indignities" and "accomplishing his fiendish purpose."

In both cases, however, there existed doubt that Nixon was the man who committed the crime, whichever version was correct. In mid-April Attorney R. H. Bagby took a petition, "numerously signed," to the governor requesting clemency on the grounds Nixon was not the right man. After Governor Mann issued a respite on April 17 to review the facts in the case, Nixon's identity was claimed to have been "clearly established," and he was taken in late May to Richmond.

No matter which story was correct, the penalty for a Black man convicted of any crime against a White woman was going to be death.

42

Byrd Jackson

BYRD JACKSON was executed on June 21, 1912, for the April assault and robbery of a Bowling Green store owner in a crime fanatically regarded by the press as "an unexampled atrocity" and "an exhibit of utmost depravity."

After entering J.L. Farmer's store, the 18-year-old Jackson pretended to be a customer, requesting an item from behind the counter. While Farmer took out the item, Jackson allegedly struck him on the head first with a brick, then an iron bar. He then took a sharp knife and "cut the man's mouth from ear to ear, then sliced off his ears, fearfully maiming and disfiguring him." Jackson then dragged the injured Farmer into a ditch by the road, leaving him all night in the rain.

Jackson took $120 from the store till and out of Farmer's pockets. He then reportedly picked up a Richmond friend named Gilton Saunders and the two had a reported "high old time" for an entire week.

When the two returned to Caroline, they were spotted, and Sheriff Gill with a posse of 25 men and a team of bloodhounds caught them after a short chase. Three White men, wrongfully arrested for the attack, were released from jail.

At his apprehension, Jackson tried to implicate Saunders in the attack on Farmer, but after his arrest, he confessed he worked alone. After a short trial on April 16, the Caroline County District Court sentenced him to death, even though Farmer was recovering from his wounds.

There have been very few executed in Virginia for assault and/or robbery without a murder. Noah Finley was hanged September 15, 1899, for robbing and shooting at (and missing) a respected White businessman in Pulaski named Major Darst. In this case, the *Richmond Planet* reported that when the jury was unable to decide after 15 hours of deliberation, "a party of citizens notified them that if a verdict was not rendered by 10:00 a.m., the negro would be lynched."

"The verdict was brought in promptly at the specified time."

Also, the *Planet* reported that on the same day Noah Finley hanged for robbery, a White Fredericksburg man named Edward Conway was found guilty of murdering a Black man, Clarence Scott "in a cold-blooded assassination." Conway was fined $10.

Some unnamed persons contended to the court in Byrd Jackson's case that since no murder was committed, he was ineligible for a death sentence. But at the time, $3674 of the criminal code provided death or from eight to 18 years for robbery under threat of murder or attempted murder. The *Alexandria Gazette* speculated correctly that "...

the Governor will not exercise the prerogative of executive clemency in this case."

NO JUSTICE IN VIRGINIA.

The Law is One=Eyed--Colored Men Receive No Protection.

THE CONSTITUTION AND ITS PROVISIONS.

A Peculiar Condition---The Two Cases--Read and Compare Them.

All persons born or naturalized in the United States and subject to the jurisdiction thereof, are citizens of the United States, and of the state wherein they reside.

No state shall make or enforce any law which shall abridge the privileges or immunities of citizens of the United States; nor shall any state deprive any person of life, liberty or property, without due process of law, nor deny to any person within its jurisdiction the Equal Protection of the Laws---XIVth Amendment to the Constitution of the United States.

A COLORED MAN HANG FOR ROBBERY.	A WHITE MAN FINED $10 FOR MURDER.
Noah Finley (colored) was charged with robbing a white man on the public highway. He was sentenced to death. The following is the telegraphic report:	"Fredericksburg, Va., Sept. 5.--Edward H. Conway (white) charged with killing Clarence Scott (colored) ended this afternoon in the County Court of Spottsylvania, the jury rendering a verdict imposing a fine of $10 on the accused."
East Radford, Va., August 8.--Noah Finley received his sentence with peculiar composure. The jury considered their verdict from Monday evening until 11 o'clock this morning.	This murder was one of the most cold blooded assassination in the history of Spottsylvania County.
The first poll stood eleven for hanging, one for eighteen years and the verdict approved by every one.	
Pulaski, Va., August 8.--It was reported the jury could not reach an agreement. A party of citizens notified them if a verdict was not rendered by 10 o'clock this morning, the Negro would be lynched. The verdict was brought in promptly at the specified time.	

Richmond Planet, Sept. 16, 1899.

43

Virginia Christian

O N AUGUST 16, 1912, on the day after her 17th birthday, Virginia Christian, a Black teenager from Elizabeth City County became the first juvenile female to be executed in the electric chair in the twentieth century. The *Richmond Planet* reported that "The usual three shocks were administered by the officer in charge of the electric current. Each time the electric switch was touched, the body of the woman responded with fearful convulsions. Death, it is believed, was instantaneous."

No other condemned woman in America could have been treated worse by the courts and the newspapers than Virginia Christian. The *Newport News Daily Press* described her as "a full-blooded negress, with kinky hair done up in threads, with dark lusterless eyes and with splotches on the skin of her face. Her color was dark brown, and her figure was short, dumpy and squashy. She had some schooling, but her speech betrayed it. Her language was the same as the unlettered members of her race."

At the age of thirteen, Christian dropped out of Hampton's Whitter Training School to work as a laundress for Ida Belote, age 52, "a frail, delicate widow who weighed no more than 91 pounds" and "mother of five fine sons and three refined daughters." Christian's parents had a long working relationship with the Belote family. Charlotte Christian (Virginia's mother) had worked for Belote when she was a young girl, and Virginia's father Henry sold fish to the Belote family.

Belote's burial in St. John's cemetery on March 21 was only the first chapter in what was described as "the most tragic, deliberate and atrocious murders that this county has ever known." Belote was considered a member of Hampton's White aristocracy by way of her father's prominence as the owner of a large grocery store.

On March 19, Ida Belote went to the Christian home to ask Virginia's mother if the girl could do some washing for her. Mrs. Christian, who had been paralyzed for years and confined to a wheelchair, was reportedly hesitant because she knew Belote frequently mistreated her daughter but told the woman she would send Virginia to her house when she returned.

Virginia went to Belote's house, and an argument erupted between the two when Belote accused Christian of stealing a locket and a skirt.

After a heated disagreement, Belote allegedly picked up and threw a ceramic cuspidor (spittoon) at the girl, hitting her on the shoulder. It fell and broke, and Belote began throwing the broken pieces. Christian rushed to protect herself, grabbing broken pieces of the spittoon and slashing at Belote.

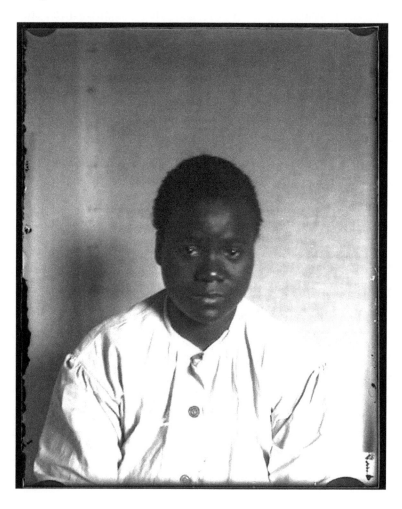

Finally, Christian and Belote both grabbed for two broom handles used to prop open windows. Christian grabbed one first and struck Belote on the forehead, knocking her to the floor. As the woman lay there screaming and bleeding from a deep cut over her ear, Christian stuffed a towel into her mouth, and using the broom handle forced the towel down her throat. Belote died by suffocation.

Christian dragged Belote's body to a back room, then returned home, busying herself with housework and telling no one what happened.

After a few hours, Belote's two youngest daughters, Eight-year-old Sadie and 13-year-old Harriet returned home from school, and after finding the front door locked, went around back, where Harriet saw her mother's body through a window, lying on the floor, surrounded by blood.

When Sheriff Curtis and Hampton police arrived at the Belote home, they reportedly found a trail of blood throughout the first floor. Overturned furniture and a shattered spittoon indicated that "a horrific struggle" had occurred.

Neighbors reported hearing no noise from the house, nor did they see anyone leave during the day.

Elizabeth City County Coroner Dr. George Vanderslice arrived at the crime scene and reported on the condition of the body:

> A bloody towel was rolled and stuffed tightly down the throat, pushing in the hair, pushing down the tongue, and inverting the lower lip. Bruises around the neck, a large cut and bruise, and black above and below one eye about the right eye, the left eye bruised swollen stuck together, finger marks around side of the neck beneath the jaw and below the ear. In addition, there

is a large cut three inches long down to the bone, just
above the left ear.

Christian was immediately suspected and police arrested her, and
after recovering a bloody waistcoat from under her bed charged her
with capital murder. During questioning without legal counsel present, she admitted to hitting Belote but expressed shock that the
woman was dead. Also, a pocketbook, ring and other valuables belonging to Belote were found on Virginia after her arrest, upping the
charges to murder in the commission of a robbery.

Christian vigorously denied that she was guilty of the murder,
claiming she had no intention of killing Belote and denied robbing her.

While confined in county jail awaiting trial, Christian – described
as "sullen and indifferent" – may have realized just how much trouble
she was in. After a sleepless night, she called for her pastor, the Rev.
J.W. Patterson, and subsequently made a full confession to the crime
in the presence of him, Elder T. H. Shorts and Sheriff R. K. Curtis. The
full text was printed in stereotype minstrel dialect in the April 11 edition of the *Times-Herald* newspaper:

> She (Belote) come to mammer's house dat morning
> an' say she want me to come an' do some washin'.
> When I come home mammer say miss Belote want me
> an' I went 'roun' to de house. I wen' in de back way an'
> when she see me she asked me about a gold locket she
> missed. I told her I ain't seen it an' don't know nuthin'
> about it. She also say sumthin' about a skirt but de
> main thing was the locket. She say "yes you got it an' if
> you don't bring it back, I'm goin' to have you put in
> jail."
>
> "I got mad an' told her if I did have it, she wasn't goin'
> to git it back. Den she picked up de spittoon and hit

me wit it an' it broke. They wuz two sticks in de room, broom handles. She run for one, an' I for de' other. I got my stick furst an' I hit her wit it 'side de hade and she fell down. She kep' hollerin' so I took a towel and stuffed it in her mouth. I helt it there twel she quit hollerin' and jes' groaned. I didn't mean to kill her an' I didn't know I had. I was mad when I hit her an' stuffed the towel in her mouth to keep her from hollerin'. I never meant to kill her. When I lef' she was groanin' and layin' on her back.

Christian's trial ran from April 1-9 and was packed every day with Black and White spectators. One juror, B. F. Elliott, was excused from the jury because he claimed to be opposed to capital punishment.

Christian never took the stand on her behalf – her Black attorneys, Joseph Thomas Newsome and George Washington Fields feared her "uncouth appearance and her insolent way of describing the deed" could incite lynch violence against local Blacks. The press reported (with no documentation or interviews) that many Hampton middle-class Blacks were equally enraged by Christian's actions, and did not view her crime as an act of self-defense against exploitative labor conditions, but an embarrassing and disgraceful offense that called for swift justice.

Since premeditation had to be proved for a first-degree murder conviction, the prosecution maintained that through "medical opinion" the towel was forced five inches down Belote's throat with the broom handle and that the time taken to accomplish this was sufficient to constitute premeditation, which under Virginia law need only be of a few minutes duration.

Despite vigorous claims of self-defense from Christian's attorneys, and with a lynch mob allegedly looming in the background, the Elizabeth City County Prosecutor fully intended to make an example out of

Christian. In a page straight from the Jim Crow handbook, he used the case to remind the local Black community that the consequences of killing a White person, especially an employer, was always death.

The jury returned a verdict of guilty of first-degree murder after 23 minutes of deliberation. Judge Clarence W. Robinson immediately sentenced her to death in the electric chair on the day after her seventeenth birthday on August 16, 1912.

On July 16, Ida Belote's brother, Lewter F. Hobbs, had sent a letter to Governor Mann, expressing confidence the courts would do their job:

> Shortly after this crime was committed, and it was known almost to a certainty that the condemned negress was the guilty party, I was notified and several of my friends suggested that a lynching was the only course to consider in the case and while I was very much wrought up still I controlled myself sufficiently to stand for the laws of the Commonwealth to have their course and this action was taken.

On July 24, 1912, former National Association of Colored Women (NACW) President Mary Church Terrell presented Governor Mann with a petition to commute Christian's sentence. The petition containing the names of over three hundred NACW members stated, in part:

> The members of the National Association of Colored Women do most earnestly implore His Excellency to commute the sentence of Virginia Christian ... The extreme youth of this girl, the lack of training during her childhood ... justifies mercy for this unfortunate girl. We feel that the electrocution of this poor girl would be repugnant to the Christian womanhood and

manhood of not only the United States but of the whole civilized world.

Soon afterward the newly-formed NAACP got involved in the Christian case, stating that:

> ... An effort should be made to save this girl's life on the ground of her age, lack of premeditation, doubt as to moral responsibility, and because of the increasing general belief that it is a disgrace to civilization for any modern State to put to death a mental child, whatever her color or race, when that child has been the product of adverse conditions for which society is to blame.

Richmond Bank President Maggie Walker also appealed to Governor Mann to commute Christian's sentence.

In early August, after Virginia was sent to the penitentiary in Richmond to await execution, Governor Mann declined to commute the death sentence, despite a personal plea from Virginia's mother, Charlotte Christian, which was published verbatim in the *Hampton Monitor*:

> My dear mr governor,
>
> Please for give me for Bowing low to write you a few lines: I am the mother of Virginiany Christian. I have been pairalized for mor then three years and I could not look after Gennie as I wants too. I know she dun an awful weaked thing when she kill Miss Belote and I hear that the people at the penetintry wants to kill her but I is praying night and day on my knees to God that he will soften your heart so that She may spend the rest of her days in prison. they say that the whole thing is in yours Hands and I know Governer if you will

onely save my child who is little over sixteen years old God will Bless you for ever ... If I was able to come to see you I could splain things to you better but I cant do nothing but pray to God and ask him to help you to simpithise with me and my truble

I am your most umble subgeck,

Charlotte Christian

Christian's father, Henry Christian also wrote on August 13, saying in part that "I told Virginia to stay away from Mrs. Belote, because Mrs. Belote was crabbed, and she surely would get in trouble. But Mrs. Belote and her children were all the time coming after her ... Virginia never gave us any trouble before this, and I believe what she said, that she was trying to defend herself."

His expressive and well-written three-page letter, transcribed by a notary, was not published.

In Chicago, Black and White social activists, business owners, and politicians sent more than 500 letters to the governor asking mercy for Christian. E. Val Putnam, Managing Editor of the *Chicago Daily World*, showed up to see the governor in person, then wrote that "never before has there been such as impassioned appeal to save a young colored girl from being electrocuted in Virginia."

W. J. Anderson, a Chicago lawyer nicknamed "Habeas Corpus" Anderson, also arrived on August 15 to plead the girl's case with the governor.

The governor remained unmoved, writing that "Christian's murder of her White employer, Ida Virginia Belote, was the most dastardly in the state's history and that Christian's execution is necessary to ensure public safety ... I have therefore reluctantly reached the conclusion that there is nothing in the case which justifies executive clemency."

Despite a brief respite due to a court paperwork error, Christian's execution day arrived. She was awakened just after 4:00 a.m. with a breakfast of eggs, biscuits, and coffee. She collapsed in her cell just before 7:00 as the death warrant was being read, but was able to walk to the execution chamber on her own. In a bizarre acquiescence to Southern propriety, the lower electrode was attached to Christian's forearm instead of to her leg.

The *Richmond Planet* remarked that "The remarkable and almost fanatical calm which characterized Virginia Christian as she was led from her cell to the chair of death is said to have deeply impressed the prison guards."

A *Lima* (Ohio) *News* reporter wrote that as Christian entered the chamber her face "was absolutely calm. She gave a quick glance at the instrument of death, more in curiosity than in fear, lowered her eyes and stepped on the platform. A guard motioned her to be seated in the chair and the negress sank into her place. Three guards hurried forward, one adjusted the knee, another strapped the woman's form into the chair, and the others clasped on the headpiece."

"A moment later the body stiffened and twisted, a wisp of sickening smoke floated through the leatherhead piece."

After the execution, Christian's body was sent to the Charles H. Jones Funeral Home in Hampton with funds provided by Richmond and Chicago political activists. On August 18, 1912, her funeral was held at the First Baptist Church.

"Virginia Christian is a sacrifice to society," *The Crisis* Magazine wrote about the Christian case. "From the unfortunate girls' tragedy, the great commonwealth, whose name by a bitter irony of fate she bears, should read its lesson. Why has not Virginia a reformatory for colored girls? Why has it not a law forbidding the execution of children of sixteen? How many more legalized murders must be committed before civilization receives an answer to these questions and grapples with those social conditions which produce Virginia Christians in a

race which obtains neither nor fair play in so many states of this union?"

44

Herbert Peyton

O N NOVEMBER 8, 1912, Herbert Peyton, a 20-year-old Black
man from King George County, died in the electric chair for
the murder of Cornelius Johnson, also Black. Johnson was
shot to death during a "massive free-for-all" at a "colored picnic" on July 4 at Rosetta, a river resort.

Several other men, all of who had reportedly "stocked up on third-
rail whiskey," were indicted in connection with the killing, including
brothers Frank and Roy Lewis, who were arrested September 18 at the
Prince William County home of their sister.

An unknown but fierce resentment existed between Peyton and
Johnson, with each during the day threatening to kill the other. Finally,
after sensing an opportunity, Peyton allegedly crept up behind Johnson and shot him with a pistol.

The *Times-Dispatch* reported September 7 that Judge Chichester
sentenced Peyton to death in the King George Courthouse following a
verdict of first-degree murder.

Peyton's defense later claimed that no premeditation had been
proven, therefore a commutation of life in prison was requested from
Governor Mann. A telegram from the Commonwealth's Attorney of
King George on November 7, however, stated unequivocally that the
murder had been "wanton, deliberate and premeditated and without
extenuation." This convinced the governor to not interfere.

The *Mathews Journal* reported that "The electrocution was conducted without mishap."

1913

45

Richard Quarles

RICHARD T. QUARLES, a 29-year-old Black man found guilty in Hanover County of criminal assault on Myrtle Rouse, a White Hanover County schoolteacher, near Ashland in May 1912 died in the electric chair on January 3, 1913.

The press reported that Quarles' assault "was an unusually brutal one." Rouse was on her way home about a mile from Ashland when the assault occurred. After several days she was reportedly still in critical condition.

Quarles would have escaped punishment completely and another innocent man would have been executed had it not been for a remarkable series of circumstances. After an angry mob with bloodhounds spent 24 hours probing every corner of the Ashland area for Rouse's assailant, another Black neighborhood resident named Eddie Cash was arrested and taken before Rouse, who "hesitantly identified him" as her assailant. Cash was then indicted and held for the grand jury based on that partial identification and some other supposedly "incriminating evidence."

With the town clamoring for a quick punishment, Cash could very well have been rushed to the electric chair had it not been for an almost identical attack on a Henrico County woman named Maggie Robinson in early June. Henrico police arrested Quarles and charged him with attempted assault as Robinson and her younger brother walked home from a neighbor. Robinson told police Quarles stepped from behind a fence and grabbed her, but her screams frightened him away.

After Quarles' arrest, Robinson and her brother were still too terrified to positively identify him, so he was ordered held in the county jail until she recovered enough to attempt an identification.

The circumstances of the Robinson assault alerted the Hanover County authorities, who were still on the lookout for a man other than Eddie Cash who more closely matched the description furnished by Rouse. A week later, both young women identified Quarles as their assailant and he was held for the grand juries of the two counties on separate charges. Cash was thankfully released.

Quarles was tried first in Hanover Court, where he was convicted of rape and sentenced to death. No Henrico trial was necessary.

46

Roy Sullivan

ROY MAXWELL SULLIVAN, "a 32-year-old White man in a composed frame of mind and ready for the end, went to his death at sunrise on February 28, 1913, in the electric chair," the *Richmond Times-Dispatch* explained in dulcet verbiage reserved for White defendants. "Spiritual consolation was given to the young man the previous evening by ministers, and he spent his final hours in quiet meditation."

Sullivan was sentenced to four years on a road crew in Norfolk in July 1912 for forging checks. On July 29 he was part of a band of 50 prisoners laying a roadbed in North Chatham, in Pittsylvania County. The force went to work that day as usual at 6:00 a.m., with some – including Sullivan – in a rock quarry and others on the roadbed.

Sullivan knew that lying partly concealed behind some loose stones in the quarry was a revolver, placed there by a Black ex-convict named Robert Womack, with whom he had somehow made previous arrangements. He got hold of the weapon about 7:00 a.m. and waited for his chance. When Guard John C. Howard's back was turned, Sullivan advanced toward him. Suddenly Howard turned, and Sullivan ordered hands up. Instead, the guard – "known for his unflinching courage" – reached for his pistol. Sullivan fired into the guard's side, then took his pistol and a rifle before disappearing into the underbrush.

Despite the quick appearance of a Dr. Perris from Chatham, Howard died about four hours later without regaining consciousness. He left a widow and a small child.

A telegram for help went out, and by 6:00 p.m. a posse of 30 men and several bloodhounds from Lynchburg, commandeered by Pittsylvania Sheriff Harvey, set out in pursuit of the escaped prisoner.

The next day the searchers discovered that Sullivan had gone to the home of an elderly Black woman near Sheva and at gunpoint demanded an ax to knock off his shackles. He told the woman as he worked that he had nothing personal against Howard, but that he was determined to escape, so he, unfortunately, had to kill him. Also, a farmer from Whittles reported to the posse that the previous evening he saw a hatless, coatless, and shoeless man with a gun walking north.

On July 31, after an incredible 55-mile pursuit through woods and forest roads, some members of the posse finally surrounded Sullivan. Chief of Police Adams, with the bloodhounds, was almost a mile away when he heard shots fired. One of the men had shot Sullivan, wounding him, although he was erroneously reported killed by the August 1, 1912 edition of the *Washington Evening Star*.

Sullivan was taken to a Roanoke hospital. He recovered rapidly, and on August 4, not realizing the seriousness of his situation, asked a guard how much time he thought would be added to his sentence for the murder of Howard. The hospital guard, knowing most likely Sullivan would go to the electric chair, reportedly just changed the subject.

Meanwhile, police arrested Robert Womack, the former inmate who planted the pistol in the quarry.

On September 24, while Sullivan continued to recover in a Danville jail, it was reported that due to positive public sympathy in Pittsylvania, his trial was moved to the Circuit Court in Richmond. Many people of that county felt that the road crew convicts were treated badly, and some did not hesitate to admit that Sullivan was justified in killing Howard because Sullivan – being White – "was made to work beside and with negro prisoners."

Sullivan's defense at his trial was alleged cruelty inflicted by the guard. The jury did not agree, and he was convicted of first-degree murder and sentenced to the electric chair. He was originally condemned to die in January, but Governor Mann respited him until February 28.

Roy M. Sullivan spent his last hours in a cell opposite Floyd and Claude Allen, the notorious Hillsville murderers.

47

Floyd Allen

48

Claude Allen

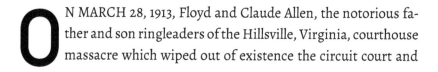

ON MARCH 28, 1913, Floyd and Claude Allen, the notorious father and son ringleaders of the Hillsville, Virginia, courthouse massacre which wiped out of existence the circuit court and

Sheriff's office of Carroll County, were put to death in the electric chair for first-degree murder.

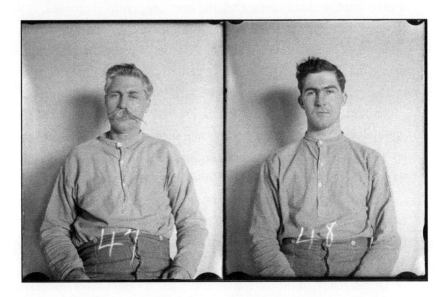

The *Roanoke Times* stated that "Not even the most pessimistic could ever have imagined, let alone believed, that such reckless disregard for human life, and such utter lack of the appreciation of home-ties, family welfare and disregard of law existed within the borders of this State, as existed in Carroll County."

Like the Confederate monuments that once highlighted Richmond's Monument Avenue, the Southern historians and authors of various songs, poems, and books of the "Hillsville Massacre" have struggled to establish control of the history of this event. The Hillsville story is ultimately a political one and is as much about the animosity between the Allen family's violent yet affluent leadership in Carroll County's Democratic Party and that of local Republicans, who in the preceding elections had finally voted the Allen's dominance out.

The Allen family had long been known as desperadoes in and around the Hillsville area, but despite local media accounts and even twenty-first-century dissertations, they were far from being rough and uneducated mountaineers. Claude Allen had even completed two years of Business College in Raleigh, North Carolina. Though they mostly kept to themselves, they became dangerous if crossed. It was claimed that some of them sold liquor illicitly from their own stills in defiance of the Commonwealth of Virginia and the United States officers, but Floyd Allen vehemently denied this, claiming he only once ran a brandy still in full compliance with Virginia law.

In January 1912, Floyd Allen interfered with two deputies, Pink Samuels and Peter Easter, in the process of arresting Sidna and Wesley Edwards, both nephews, for fighting and disturbing a Primitive Baptist Church meeting. While the officers were taking the nephews to jail, Floyd Allen and one of his cousins passed by, and, believing their situation was humiliating, forcibly rescued the prisoners from the officers, beating one of the deputies and forcing the other to flee. Floyd Allen then personally took the two boys to jail and paid their bail.

On March 13, in the Carroll County Circuit Court, after several continuances (the final one on account that officer Pink Samuels had been scared out of the State by the Allens), Floyd Allen was prosecuted for interfering with a police officer in the discharge of his duty. Rumor had it that Allen made many threats toward the judge and the court officers. The judge had even been advised to go to the courthouse armed, but he emphatically stated that he would not "so demean his office as judge as to wear a pistol while sitting on the bench."

Allen was quoted by several witnesses as saying that if he were convicted, he would "make the biggest hole in that court that any man ever made." He was further quoted as saying that if the judge would not do his duty he would "pile him up with the rest of them."

After all the evidence was heard, the court adjourned for the day. Locals had good reason to be concerned about trying Floyd Allen, as he had endured numerous legal issues since 1889 and always seemed to escape them with little or no punishment.

Early the next morning, Floyd and many of his family members showed up at the courthouse. The entire gang, with their sympathizers, were permitted in the courtroom, loaded down with guns and bolts filled with cartridges which had been openly and knowingly shipped in beforehand. Knowing the men, and their reputations, it seems inconceivable that they allowed so many guns inside the courtroom. It was rumored that the officers knew the men were armed but because of the Allen's status, they were afraid to disarm them.

The jury was sent to deliberate, while the court, with Judge Thornton L. Massie on the bench, took up other business. Finally, the jury returned and rendered a verdict of guilty, with a recommended punishment of one year's confinement in the State Penitentiary. There was a moment of silence before Judge Massle declared: "Sheriff, take charge of the prisoner."

Allen then supposedly stood and exclaimed to Judge Massie "If you sentence me on that verdict, I will kill you."

Unintimidated, Judge Massie proceeded to affirm the jury's recommendation. Sheriff Lewis F. Webb left his stand in front of the clerk's desk and took a step toward Allen when he fumbled inside his sweater, and announced, "Gentlemen, I ain't a-goin."

Floyd Allen then allegedly pulled a pistol and fired toward Judge Massie. Almost immediately Sheriff Webb drew his gun and shot Floyd, wounding him. But then other members of the Allen family opened fire with revolvers and there followed a scene of carnage "the likes of which no other courtroom in the world ever witnessed."

It was a free-for-all of deafening gunshots, smoke, terror, and panic. Members of the Allen clan mercilessly shot down one court officer and members of the jury after another, while many spectators were wounded by flying bullets. In the pandemonium, it was impossible to tell who was shooting and who was being shot.

Floyd Allen fell to the floor, falsely claiming he had been shot in the groin. However, he quickly arose and fired several more times. Claude and Sidna Allen advanced and initiated a pistol duel with the officers of the court. Floyd's nephew Wesley Edwards fired from near the stove on the north side of the room. Friel Allen fired from the steps to the jury room on the west side at Court Clerk Dexter Goad, and Floyd Allen and Wesley Edwards each shot at Woodson Quisenberry, the deputy clerk of the court, who returned fire, along with several deputy sheriffs.

The population of the courtroom spilled into the street, followed by the Allens, who continued firing at the remaining jurors as they fled through the town. The Allens, however, were not expecting Goad, who, with all his fellow court officers dead, and despite a wound to his neck, followed the Allens outside and blasted away at them. He managed to wound Sidna and Floyd Allen outside the courthouse despite also being shot in the legs.

In addition to Judge Massie (who lived for almost a half-hour, saying with his dying breath that he was shot by Sidna Allen, not Floyd), Sheriff Webb and Commonwealth's Attorney William M. Foster were killed. A juror named Fowler died two days later without regaining consciousness. Goad was initially reported as killed but was badly wounded, shot through the neck. Also wounded were Ridney Allen, brother of Floyd; jurors Faddie and C. Caine; and court spectators A.T. Howlett, Bruce Marshall, and Stuart Worrell.

After the shooting, the unwounded Allen clan members took charge of Hillsville, shooting up the town and terrorizing the inhabitants. They finally left, except for Floyd, who was too badly wounded to travel, and his son Victor, who remained with him inside the Hillsville Hotel.

Residents quickly telegraphed the news to Governor Mann in Richmond: "Judge Massie shot dead on the bench, commonwealth shot dead at the bar, the sheriff shot dead in courthouse, several others wounded, help wanted."

By law, if a sheriff was killed, the deputies lost their status, so for a brief period, Carroll County was without any law enforcement – meaning Floyd and Victor were taken into custody early the following morning by regular citizens.

Richmond was stunned by this unbelievable event, and military companies prepared to go to Hillsville, but Governor Mann decided instead to send detectives to scour the mountains for the fleeing outlaws. He immediately wired W. G. Baldwin of the Baldwin-Felts Detective Agency in Roanoke to "take such men as you think may be necessary and proceed at once to Hillsville and arrest murderers and all connected with the crime. Spare no expense."

Numerous surrounding counties also sent in officers and volunteers, led by the Baldwin-Felts detectives, to restore order and comb the mountains for the fugitives.

On April 5, a Mount Airy, North Carolina man named Sug Smith told an Associated Press reporter that Sidna Edwards and Wesley Edwards came to his cabin begging for food. Aware that the Virginia governor had posted bills stating no one was to render aid to the fugitives, Smith refused to help them and they went to the mountains. Exhausted and hungry, they surrendered a week later.

Claude Allen was caught by detectives in hiding two weeks after the shootings. Friel Allen was turned in through the intervention of his father. Six months from the day of the shooting, Sidna Allen and Wesley Edwards were finally captured in Des Moines, Iowa. Detectives learned of their whereabouts after Wesley could not resist sneaking home to Carroll County for a discreet visit.

Upon their arrests, the Allen family claimed that several court officials opened fire first on Floyd Allen, while other witnesses contended that Claude Allen, the defendant's son, initiated the shooting. Nevertheless, from April through December 1912, Floyd Allen, Claude Allen, and other members of the Allen family were tried for murder in the Wythe County Circuit Court.

In a special session beginning April 30, the court first tried Floyd for the murder of Sheriff Foster. Floyd defended himself by claiming that clerk Dexter Goad had a gun ready and was partnered with the sheriff to kill him, but this argument failed to influence the jury. The prosecution argued that the Allens had conspired to shoot the court officers if Floyd received a jail sentence, and the jury found this argument more convincing. Floyd Allen was convicted of first-degree murder on May 16, 1912.

His son Claude was tried first for killing Judge Massie. He swore to have fired only at Goad and only then in defense when he saw Goad trying to shoot his father. Convicted of second-degree murder, he received 15 years imprisonment. He was then tried for killing Sheriff Webb, resulting in a hung jury. His third trial, for killing juror Fowler convicted him of first-degree murder and a sentence of death.

Sidna Allen, Floyd's brother and considered the most dangerous of the Allens, was sentenced to 35 years in the penitentiary for second-degree murder and voluntary manslaughter. Sidna Edwards, nephew of Floyd and Sidna Allen, plead guilty to second-degree murder and received 15 years in the penitentiary. Friel Allen, Floyd's nephew, confessed to shooting the commonwealth's attorney and received 18 years in the penitentiary for second-degree murder. Wesley Edwards, brother of Sidna Edwards, received a 27-year prison sentence – 18 years for two counts of first-degree murder and nine years for second-degree murder.

There was a brief movement in Carroll County to secure the death penalty for Sidna Allen, but commute the same penalty for Claude and Floyd Allen to life imprisonment, since in the utter confusion of the courtroom fusillade it was impossible to ascertain exactly who shot whom. The Supreme Court refused to hear the case, even though petitions to commute Claude gathered an incredible 75,000 signatures, from such people and organizations as industrial workplaces, Sunday school classes, Washington and Lee University, the University of

Virginia law school and retail businesses. Richmond women called for petitions from other women around the state. Money was raised and contributed to pay the expenses of presenting appeals to Governor Mann.

Governor Mann granted three respites while appeals were filed, but believed if he commuted Claude Allen's sentence, then his personal life, his political future, even his "fate after death" were all threatened. He released a statement on March 6 denying the commutation of the death sentences.

The Allens' attorneys then sought a hearing from the U.S. Supreme Court, who refused to hear the case. On March 12 Governor Mann sent a letter to the injured Dexter Goad, praising him for firing back at the Allens that day.

> "... you had the nerve to follow these men out of the courthouse and continue firing although wounded ... shows that your veins are filled with the red blood of Virginia ancestors and that the state has a right to and can confidently expect of the citizens of Carroll every effort for the capture and punishment of the men who have defiled the laws of Virginia. I have entire confidence in the manhood of a county which has such a citizen and officer as yourself."

The Allens denied that they had conspired to kill the court officers. In a final statement on March 27, 1913, Floyd stated that "a great injustice has been done" and that he was the victim of a political plot to kill him. "I believe that the attempt on my life was made for no other cause except for my active work in the Democrat[ic] party and the bitter feeling that had gotten up between Dexter Goad and others on account of my work for the party."

On execution day the men awoke with the full expectation of dying within an hour or two. Floyd Allen "feared he would break down, but he remained entirely composed." Claude awoke a little later and began to sing. "I'm Going Home, to Die No More."

After a short time, the guards came and read the death warrants. Claude agreed that his father should go first, saying, "He has grieved more about me than I have about myself." Floyd was taken from his cell and walked to his younger son, holding out his hand. "Good-bye father," Claude said. "I hope we will meet in a happier land."

"I think we will," replied the father. "I know we will," he repeated in a positive, almost buoyant tone. A moment later he entered the door to the death chamber. When the guards returned, Claude turned willingly to them and stated he was ready to go. He clasped the ministers and told them good-bye. The *Times-Dispatch* claimed, "they maintained a stiff upper lip until he had gone through the door, then reportedly broke down in tears."

The bodies of the two men were sent by train back to Hillsville, and on March 30, over 5,000 people, mostly from Grayson, Wythe, and Carroll Counties, attended their funerals. Immediately following brief messages by Primitive Baptist preachers, the caskets were opened at their burial spot in a field on a ridge and for over an hour people filed past, viewing the bodies. Then they were buried side by side.

A plaque over Claude Allen's grave reads "Sacred to the Memory of Claude S. Allen and his father, Who was judicially murdered in the Va. Penitentiary March 28, 1913 by order of the Governor of the State over the protest of 100000 Citizens of the State of Va."

49

James Goode

J AMES GOODE, *alias* Joe Jones, *alias* "Midnight," age 28, went to death in the electric chair May 16, 1913, for the murder of Julius Smith, a Newport News merchant and Russian immigrant. Smith was robbed of about $100 then "brutally beaten" with an iron pike at his Jefferson Avenue store on January 20 of that year.

He lingered for about a week before he died without regaining consciousness.

Goode fled the city after the attack, but on January 21 his parents, who lived in Chesterfield, called Petersburg police when they found out their son was wanted by the Norfolk police. Goode gave them $50.35, some of it blood-stained, telling them he had earned it in New York. The parents promptly handed it all over to the police.

On January 26 another merchant named Mendel Finkelstein positively identified Goode as the Black man who assaulted him and ransacked his shoe store three weeks earlier. According to Finkelstein, Goode forced open the door and struck him on the head with a blunt instrument, supposedly an iron bar similar to the one he used to kill Smith. Finkelstein claimed he got a good look at his assailant and was positive it was Goode.

While waiting in Richmond's Main Street station for a train to Newport News, Goode confessed to the crimes to Detective Samuel Pearson, but he also implicated Robert Bates, another Black man, claiming that Bates had killed Smith. Also, Goode confessed that he and Bates planned to rob and murder three more victims.

While on the train, Goode reportedly asked Pearson the status of the Allen gang case before suddenly asking "How long does it take a man to die in the chair?"

"Perhaps a minute," Pearson replied. The secrecy behind the electric chair was always a source of curious inquiry.

"They tell me that when a man gets into the chair that he is sure to die."

Pearson answered, "Yes I suppose he is."

Pearson reported that Goode then laid his head on the seat and slept for a half-hour.

The *Newport News Daily Press* reported that when the train arrived in that city about 5:30 p.m. there was a "great mob of negroes" who police claimed, "planned to take the prisoner from the officer and lynch him at the depot."

They had been tricked – Pearson and Goode took an earlier train and arrived at 1:30 p.m., giving Pearson plenty of time to get Goode safely to jail. At 5:00, the predicted mob arrived at the station but when they found out Goode was already in jail they dispersed.

Bates was acquitted by a jury March 12 when it was proven that Goode told fellow prisoners in the city jail that he alone was guilty.

Before 22-year-old Julius Smith died, his condition was described in agonizing detail in the *Daily Press*. "The entire top of his skull is crushed, and his brains are protruding through the wounds," the article explicitly declared. A doctor named Knight claimed that Smith would never regain consciousness, but that "he may live for some time." Smith died three days after this article was published, on January 27, 1913. The cause of death on his death certificate was listed as "Effects of blows to the head."

Because of an epidemic of smallpox in Newport News, especially in a Black community called "The Acre," Judge Brown ordered the court officers "to keep all negroes out of the courtroom."

On March 12 the jury came back after 42 minutes with a verdict of guilty of first-degree murder.

50

Alfred Wright

O N MAY 16, 1913, 18-year-old Alfred Wright died in the electric chair for the June 28, 1912 rape of a White Appomattox County woman named Bertha Ferguson. She had been in Appomattox City selling berries and was allegedly attacked at knifepoint on her way home.

"Not since the surrender has Appomattox been as greatly disturbed as it was yesterday when one of the most atrocious crimes in its history took place within a half-mile of the town ..." screamed a front-page story in the June 29, 1912, *Staunton Daily Leader*.

After notice of the attack spread, several posses of men set out in search of the culprit. Some claimed to have seen a "negro boy" plowing nearby, and when the posse arrived the boy had mounted a plow-horse and according to the press was "making a vigorous attempt to escape." He was taken into custody by a crowd and hauled before Ferguson, who identified him as her attacker. "He strongly denies his guilt," the *Daily Leader* article continued, warning however that "... the evidence is said to be complete."

Once Wright was taken to the Appomattox jail around noon, a guard of armed farmers was added to security to protect the prisoner from a lynching by an enraged mob.

On Saturday, June 29 Judge George Hundley began summoning a jury for a trial starting the next day estimated by the press as "expected to last only a few minutes." Meanwhile, more incensed neighbors continued to surround the jail, threatening a lynching.

The trial took place Monday, July 1. After about an hour of testimony from Ferguson and her brother, who allegedly witnessed the attack, the jury returned a verdict of guilty of criminal assault after about 10 minutes of deliberation. Wright was then sentenced to die in the electric chair, 48 hours after the commission of the crime.

VIRGINIA SHOWS HOW TO PREVENT RULE OF MOB

Apppomattox, July 2.—When the jury filed back into the court room here after being out 12 minutes and announced that Alfred Wright, colored, was guilty of criminally assaulting Mrs. Thomas Ferguson, last Thursday morning, fixing his penalty at death, the record of speedy justice at the hands of the courts of the commonwealth, was equaled if not surpassed. It was only 49 hours from the consummation of his crime until the negro was on trial for his life.

But the case got complicated. The zealous speed with which Wright was tried, convicted, and sentenced showed according to his attorney Duncan Drysdale, "great prejudice in the county against him." Judge Hundley ruled, however, that the prisoner's feeling that he will not get a fair trial was insufficient, and that specific proof was necessary before a verdict rendered under such circumstances could be set aside.

Attorney Drysdale fought tooth and nail for his client, entering numerous writs of error on Wright's behalf. He in turn received stay after stay, with Drysdale correctly citing "inflamed public opinion" as grounds for reversal. Adding to the confusion, Wright confessed to the crime, then sought to retract his confession.

The case wound through the courts until March 13, 1913, when the Supreme Court of Appeals upheld the verdict and the sentence of the Appomattox Circuit Court.

51

Frank Hargrove

A 39-YEAR-OLD "NEGRO GIANT" named Frank L. Hargrove died on June 20, 1913, in the electric chair for the murders of Mansfield and Melvina Thornton, a Black Spotsylvania couple. Believing there was a large sum of money inside their home, he allegedly killed them on December 12, 1912, then set the house on fire by to cover the crime. The bodies were found in the ruins.

Hargrove had the distinction at the time of being the largest man ever confined in the Henrico County Jail. "A veritable giant, he stood six feet six and one-half inches in his stocking feet," reported the *Richmond Times-Dispatch*, "and tipped the scales at 240 pounds, with not one ounce of superfluous fat. He was perfectly proportioned, and towered over his guards."

Fredericksburg Sergeant Chichester arrested Hargrove for suspicion of being connected to the crime when he was seen wearing bloodstained clothes. George Scott, a Black Fredericksburg man, was also arrested and held as a possible suspect.

During his February 14-19, 1913 trial, Hargrove strenuously denied his guilt under questioning by Commonwealth's Attorney T. Stokely Coleman, but later out of desperation, decided to cop an insanity plea. The next day he arrived at the courtroom, raving and in ripped clothing, forcing guards to tie him to his chair. Several prisoners in the Henrico jail with him testified, however, that he offered them money to say he was crazy. Coleman made a convincing argument that Hargrove's pretensions to insanity were "glaring frauds."

> # COUNTY JAIL HAS GIANT IN CUSTODY
>
> ---
>
> Negro Murderer, Behind Its Bars, Is 6 Feet 6 1-2 Inches Tall.

A press reporter noted that Hargrove's insanity must have been faked, as he was spotted talking in a normal tone with his attorney after the verdict had been read.

The trial established that on December 12 Hargrove arrived at the Thornton home, then called Mansfield Thornton outside where they began to loudly argue. Alerted by the voices, Thornton's wife Melvina came out, and Hargrove "crushed both their skulls with a club." He reportedly carried them inside to a bed, ransacked the house looking for the money, then set the house on fire on his way out.

Despite his "pretensions to insanity" and his claims of innocence, one notable piece of evidence seemed to point to Hargrove's guilt: James Thornton, the father of the murdered man, testified that the afternoon before the murder, Hargrove gave him a drink of whiskey out of a peculiarly marked bottle. A bottle matching that description was later found where the murder occurred, and "was proven in court to be the same bottle of which Thornton took the drink given him by Hargrove a few hours previous to the murder."

The jury returned with a verdict of guilty of premeditated murder after 15 minutes of deliberation and sentenced Hargrove to die in the electric chair. In an appeal to the governor, Hargrove explained that the blood on his clothes was the result of killing hogs for a neighboring farmer; however, an inquiry proved that no hog butchering was done on the day he claimed. He also floated a claim of mistaken identity, to no avail. George Scott was released upon Hargrove's conviction.

The Hargrove case was the first verdict of premeditated murder in Spotsylvania County in over 40 years. According to the June 17 *Richmond Times-Dispatch*, "[The conviction and sentence] met with such universal approval that the governor saw no need to interfere with the judgment."

52

Nelson Carter

ON JUNE 27, 1913, Nelson V. Carter, a White resident of Spotsylvania County, was electrocuted for the February 6 murder of his wife, Hattie B. Carter, remembered as a "greatly beloved woman."

Hattie separated from her husband, citing cruelty and abuse, and for a while lived in Richmond with their oldest daughter. Through the mediation of friends, however, they reconciled and she moved back to their home near Fredericksburg. Press reports stated that while pending divorce suits had been withdrawn by both of them, they continued to quarrel.

On the day of the murder, Nelson Carter ate breakfast at his father's home about a mile away. Upon returning he met Hattie inside their house, and they again began to quarrel. He then drew a pistol and reportedly shot her through the mouth. She fled out into the yard, with her husband pursuing her and pouring four more shots into her. She had just reached the yard gate after the sixth shot when she fell.

While in jail, Carter declared that he deliberately shot his wife to kill her and that he would do so again under similar circumstances. The Associated Press reported that the commonwealth's attorney requested a speedy trial, "as the people of the county were greatly wrought up over this most atrocious and unprovoked murder."

Carter pleaded homicidal insanity, yet despite a brief delay during the trial when a juror was diagnosed with measles, he was found guilty, sentenced to death, and placed in the Fredericksburg jail to await transport to the State Penitentiary.

While in jail, one of Carter's five daughters, Florence Carter, married a Richmond man named Lee Coleman. She was only 14 years of age, so the court appointed a special guardian to give consent to the marriage, since her father, being a convicted felon awaiting execution, was legally unable to give consent.

On June 11 the Supreme Court of Virginia declined to grant a writ of error.

After Carter's execution, his body was claimed by relatives, and shipped to Spotsylvania for burial.

53

Owen Goggin

OWEN COGGIN, a 36-year-old Black Bedford County farmhand, "paid the extreme penalty of the law" on June 27, 1913, for a "criminal attack" on a well-liked Joppa Mills post office secretary and farm owner, Julia Reese "Ras" Nance. He was executed immediately after Nelson Carter.

Nance and a young child (erroneously referred to in press reports as a son, but Nance never married and had no children), were sitting down to lunch at 1:00 p.m. on March 20, when Goggin, a family employee, came inside. Knowing Nance was alone, Goggin reportedly saw an opportunity to rob the house. He grabbed an ax by the fireplace and struck the 35-year-old woman over the head with the flat side, knocking her to the floor. In the commotion, the 7-year-old boy ran off to find help.

Goggin had no idea what he was in for. Thinking he had killed the woman or at least knocked her unconscious, he dropped the ax and turned to go upstairs. Nance, however, got up, grabbed the ax and rushed toward Goggin, chopping and slashing repeatedly at his head and chest. At one point she embedded the ax deep in his shoulder then wrenched it out before he could get out the door, screaming in agony and bleeding profusely from several deep gashes. Nance then bounded up the steps, grabbed a pistol from her room, and fired twice at Goggin as he staggered down the road but neither bullet struck him.

Soon afterward, neighbors alerted by the boy arrived and took off in pursuit of the badly injured Goggin. When they caught up with him, he was in shock, covered in blood, and offered no resistance. He was held until Bedford City police officers took him to jail.

Despite rumors that Goggin's terrible injuries were possibly fatal, an angry crowd still surrounded the jail demanding a lynching, but armed guards stood firm throughout the night. The crowd eventually one by one "melted away."

The press reported that Nance "received quite a shock to her nervous system by the attack," but she fully recovered. There was no mention of medical attention Goggin may have received.

The Bedford County Court convened at 10:00 a.m. on April 10, with Roanoke Judge Waller Staples presiding since Bedford Judge Campbell was ill that day. The *Richmond Times-Dispatch* observed that "The courthouse was filled with townspeople, and many from the nearby country districts, who came to witness the swift action of the court of bringing the assailant of Mrs. [sic] Nance to justice." Seeing the writing on the wall, court-appointed defense attorney London Lowry called a few friendly witnesses in the hopes of "securing a lesser verdict than death in the chair." It was a moot point, as "sturdy farmers and businessmen sat in judgment" and by their appearances, they were going to vote for death in any case.

Goggin was convicted of criminal assault and sentenced to death after only a few minutes of deliberation. He was sent to the Lynchburg jail as a safety precaution until his transportation to Richmond. One respite was granted by Governor Mann on June 5 to consider an application for commutation, but it was denied.

Julia "Ras" Nance, the tough-as-nails post office employee, later retired and died of a stroke on December 2, 1944, at age 65.

54

Benjamin Baily

BENJAMIN BAILY, a Black, intellectually disabled Northern Virginia native, was executed on August 8, 1913. The 23-year-old was convicted in Fairfax of a May 22 criminal assault on the 6-year-old daughter of Gabriel Fallin, a well-known farmer, near Great Falls.

In alarmingly familiar language describing crimes like this, the *Alexandria Gazette* howled that the case was "a crime so horrible in its details that officers of the court, hardened to many a pitiful story in the course of their work, shuddered as the facts were told at Fairfax Courthouse today ..."

Baily eluded capture for five days until he was arrested on May 27 by Constable Owen Daily, and the next day, May 28, he was indicted by a special grand jury after only a few minutes deliberation, entering a plea of not guilty. The press noted that even though he made a "complete confession," he "seemed to be half-witted and did not understand the few questions that were put to him."

To prevent a possible lynching, his trial was set for two days later, on May 30. Baily was tried, convicted, and sentenced to die, only eight days after his crime. One potential juror, a man ironically named Vernon Lynch, was excused when he explained that he was opposed to capital punishment.

The case occupied only two hours of the court's time. Baily's elementary-age victim was the principal witness against him. He denied the charge, "but his testimony was badly shaken on the stand on cross-examination."

The jury was out about "10 or 12" minutes. Foreman Philip Ward then stood and read, "We the jury find the prisoner Benjamin Baily *alias* Ben Baily guilty of rape as charged in the within indictment and ascertain his punishment to be death."

The *Gazette* claimed that "[Baily's] speedy trial will probably never be equaled in Virginia" although that claim can be disputed by many Black-on-White trials.

On July 25 Baily was granted a respite from Governor Mann to "investigate the mental condition of the prisoner." The reason was that Baily (likely with the help of the jailer) wrote a letter to his mother, telling her that he "is well," and that he is to be "electrocuted, whatever that means." He added at the end that he wished they would "make haste and do it" because "he wants to get back home."

The sentencing stood.

55

William Glinn

WILLIAM GLINN, *alias* C. Brown, a 26-year-old Black Norfolk native, died in the electric chair on August 16, 1913, at 7:14 a.m.

Glinn was convicted of first-degree murder in Norfolk on July 3. A motion for a new trial was overruled.

There is no information available on his crime, the victim, or the trial.

56

Minnie Collins

ON OCTOBER 31, 1913, at 7:30 a.m., Minnie Collins, an 18-year-old Black farmhand from Northampton County, was executed at the State Penitentiary for the attempted rape of an unknown White woman.

Almost nothing is known of this case, other than the Northampton County Circuit Court convicted and sentenced Collins. Collins' attorney moved to set aside the jury verdict on grounds that it was "contrary to laws and evidence" but was overruled. After the trial, the Northampton sheriff transferred Collins to the Norfolk jail, for fear of a Northampton lynch mob.

After execution, his body was removed to Charlottesville.

57

Lee Archer

LEE ARCHER was a 22-year-old Black man convicted of raping Cora Whitehurst, daughter of Henry T. Whitehurst, a prosperous farmer of Bayside in Princess Anne County. He was electrocuted December 5, 1913, at the penitentiary after the Supreme Court of Appeals refused to interfere in the case.

The attack allegedly occurred September 2 at the Whitehurst home, where 19-year-old Cora was alone while her father and brothers worked on a neighboring farm. They reportedly found her unconscious upon their return, triggering an all-night search by the sheriff and a posse. Archer was captured on September 4. Despite being "in a precarious condition, under the care of physicians," Whitehurst "positively identified" Archer. He was then taken to the Princess Anne jail.

On September 5, law enforcement rushed Archer "by automobile" to the Norfolk County jail for safekeeping after Commonwealth's Attorney Ackiss learned of a potential mob forming to storm the jail and lynch the prisoner. The lynching threat also prompted Circuit Court Judge B. White to immediately call a special grand jury to indict Archer so a "speedy trial could follow."

On September 8, a mere six days after the crime, a jury convicted Archer of rape. On September 15 Judge White sentenced him to death. The *Alexandria Gazette* reported he was executed for the "usual crime," a common phrase from the period.

After execution, his body was sent to the Anatomical Board at the Medical College.

58

Newell Walker

JUST AFTER THE ELECTROCUTION of Lee Archer, Newell Walker, a White man aged 29, also went to the electric chair on December 5, 1913, for the murder of his wife, Mary Weaver Walker. Originally sentenced to die November 21, Governor Mann had granted a final two-week respite as he was reportedly "so moved by the personal pleas of the condemned man's aged mother."

The governor also considered several petitions requesting commutation of the sentence, but ultimately declined to interfere.

The press described Walker's crime in characteristic verbiage as "one of the most brutal murders of which the human mind can conceive." Charles City County neighbors and friends knew of the Walker couple and their three children's domestic troubles. Mary Walker had earlier in the year left to live with friends, stating at the time that her husband had beaten her and threatened her life over his jealousy of a boarder living at their home. Also, she had consulted a Williamsburg divorce attorney named Henley and allegedly told him she feared for her life around her husband.

On Sunday, May 18, about a mile west of Binns Hall, Newell met Mary near their house as she walked with friends and asked her in front of several people if she would come back and live with him. After she forcefully answered no, Newell "produced a straight razor and slashed her throat from ear to ear ..."

As the horrified witnesses attended to the dying woman, Newell walked into his home, washed his blood-stained hands, then called the county sheriff and surrendered.

Mary was the daughter of John Weaver, of New Kent County, and was well-respected in their neighborhood. She married Newell Walker in 1903, but their married life was very unhappy, "as her husband failed to provide for her and their three children." Newell was a jealous spouse, and the sudden violence toward his wife was not a surprise to many who knew them.

The prosecution claimed the murder had been premeditated, but while Walker acknowledged killing his wife, he claimed to have committed it in a moment of insanity.

On August 17, "in the gloomy corridor of the Henrico County jail," Walker's seven-year-old daughter, Mary, came to visit for the first time. Just before the girl's visit, the *Richmond Times-Dispatch* reported that the prisoners participated in a song and prayer service with some traveling evangelists, and Walker, "whose mental condition for the previous few weeks had been precarious, got worked up to a high nervous pitch, and the sight of family was more than he could stand." Grasping his child, and with tears pouring down his cheeks, he planted kiss after kiss on her face. After her short visit, Walker reportedly paced the prison corridor for hours, sobbing hysterically.

Sadly, after the death of their mother, the children were separated into separate households. Mary was living with an aunt in Newport News, and that was her first and only visit with her father. The other two children chose not to visit or were not allowed.

Allegedly ready to die for the crime, Walker seemed more concerned for the welfare of his children and his mother. "I am ready to go anywhere they say," he told the *Times-Dispatch*, "but who will take care of my poor old mother and my babies?"

Despite his three respites from the governor, the Supreme Court of appeals refused to hear his case.

Usually, whenever a White man and a Black man were scheduled for execution on the same day, it was customary for the White to go first. In this case, however, it seems on December 5, 1913, Lee Archer, the Black man, went first.

1914

59

Charlton Moore

CHARLTON MOORE, a 54-year-old Black Acquinton farmer, was executed in the electric chair at 7:30 a.m. on January 16, 1914, for the October 8, 1913 murder of his wife, Hannah Moore. "The man went to his death unflinchingly," claimed the *Alexandria Gazette*, "and confident that his crime would be forgiven by his maker."

A reported result of jealousy, this crime of passion was committed in King William County. The trial took an unheard-of five days, but when sentenced by the court Moore suddenly confessed the entire offense. He received no respites, and there were no appeals.

Rev. W.H. Stokes and Rev. Scott Burrell, local Black ministers, were described as constant visitors while Moore was in the death cell. His several grown children took possession of his body.

60

William Rhodes

WILLIAM "WILLIE" RHODES, a Black male aged 27, was executed January 30, 1914, for the first-degree murder of Sam Morton, who was described as one of the kindly, "old-time, well-to-do negroes" of Charlotte County. Rhodes and his girlfriend Allie Carter had moved to Charlotte the previous summer looking for work when they boarded with Morton. They later discovered that a sum of money was allegedly hidden in his house.

One day Morton and his horse and wagon disappeared. After a multi-day hunt, searchers found his battered body buried in a shallow grave in a washout.

Rhodes and Carter were suspected but had fled. In Brookneal, they sold the horse and wagon to a man who told police they claimed to be going to Roanoke, where they were eventually captured. Carter quickly confessed to the police that she alone killed Morton, but Rhodes maintained his innocence.

The police were skeptical of Carter's confession, however, as her story did not coincide with many facts in the case. Still, she and Rhodes were tried and sentenced to death at Charlotte Courthouse.

Friends of the condemned couple made vigorous appeals for the commutation of their death sentences, but the governor was not willing to consider them. Allie Carter was thus on her way to being the first woman to be executed since Virginia Christian.

On January 28, two days before her execution, Governor Mann met with Charlotte Commonwealth's Attorney Watkins after looking more closely into Carter's role in Morton's murder. In one petition, signed by many citizens of Carter's hometown of Drake's Branch, they claimed she was "mentally weak and not always responsible for her actions." She was described as a "kind-hearted, easy-going woman," and they all agreed that she "must have been drawn into the murder under Rhodes' influence." Many thought she had no actual hand in the murder at all, but consented to be made the scapegoat for her companion, Rhodes.

The governor commuted her sentence to life imprisonment.

61

Marion Lee

THIRTY-NINE-YEAR-OLD Black Charles City native Marion Lee was executed for murder on March 19, 1914. Richmond police caught Lee after he killed another Black man, Delaware Brown, following an argument over a game of cards near Toano in late December 1913. The *Newport News Daily Press* noted, "They had been in Newport News and came up together Saturday morning well loaded with booze."

He was tried and sentenced in Williamsburg.

On January 26, Governor Mann discovered that Lee's execution had to be delayed over a court error. After being found guilty of first-degree murder, the trial judge granted a stay of 40 days while the Supreme Court of Appeals reviewed Lee's case. The court refused to hear the case, but the clerk neglected to send a notice to the Williamsburg Court. Since the time extended by the judge passed the deadline, the original execution date came and went, resulting in Lee being still alive and in prison but technically "dead."

Lee was then "refused admission to the State Penitentiary" and had to remain in the James City jail to be called up a second time by the trial judge to be resentenced.

Again, he received a sentence of death.

62

Walter Boyd

WALTER BOYD, a 24-year-old Black Richmond resident, was electrocuted March 27, 1914, for the shooting death of Benjamin Franklin, also Black, the previous December 13, 1913.

Franklin, who lived at 611 Leigh Street in Richmond, was shot to death in an alley near Munford and Catherine Streets after arguing with Boyd over his wife. She told the police that Franklin came to their home on West Duval Street early on the 13th, while her husband was away and insulted her. According to her statement, when Boyd later returned, she told him what had happened. He left the house, bought a shotgun, and went out looking for Franklin.

After encountering Franklin in that alley, Boyd unloaded a load of birdshot into his left side. Franklin then staggered nearly a block before he collapsed. Someone called the City Hospital ambulance and Dr. Robert Whitehead responded, rendering emergency treatment while notifying the Second St. Police Station of the incident. Franklin was taken to the hospital, where he died.

Richmond Detectives Wiley and Kellam waited all night at Boyd's home for him to show up to arrest him. When he failed to show, his wife told them that he had a friend, called "Hessie," who lived on West Moore Street and that maybe he could tell them where he was.

The detectives were inside Hessie's home questioning him when someone knocked on the door. Hessie answered and two Black men entered. "That's him!" Hessie cried, pointing to Boyd, who was "paralyzed in fear and could not move" at the sight of the policemen. His unnamed companion, however, got away.

On January 26 Boyd became the first man sentenced to death by Judge Richardson in the Hustings Court after his conviction of first-degree murder. "And now you must begin from this moment to make your peace with God," Richardson told him at sentencing. "There is practically no hope for you here on earth. I commend you to your Heavenly Judge. May God have mercy on your soul."

An "ineffectual attempt" to commute Boyd's sentence was ignored by Governor Henry Stuart.

63

George Woods

A BLACK DANVILLE MAN named George Woods died at daybreak on May 22, 1914, in the electric chair for strangling his wife, Maria Woods and throwing her body into the Dan River. A last-minute attempt by Woods' friends to stay the execution under the pretext that he was insane was ignored, as the May 23 *Richmond Times-Dispatch* related that prison physicians "reported Woods to be above the normal negro intelligence."

Woods allegedly accosted Maria as she returned home with a friend from her job at one of Danville's tobacco factories on the north side of the city. Maria's body was later found by a man named Walter Norris, who spotted a hand "protruding from the icy waters of the Dan River."

Her body showed evidence of a struggle, and there were noticeable bruises on her throat.

Originally, the 24-year-old barber from Jacksonville, Florida was sentenced for a short term to a chain gang in Southern Virginia for retailing liquor without a license. He escaped from that gang on January 12, then went after his wife for unknown reasons, strangling her then disposing of her body in the river.

After the murder, he went to his brother's house, who refused to let him in. He was then later discovered at a "negro shanty" about a mile from the home of Constable Thomas. He confessed to murdering his wife before affecting insanity.

"He did not seem to realize the gravity of his offense," stated the *Richmond Times-Dispatch*, "and attributed no motive for the crime."

After being locked up, and seeing that the insanity defense was going nowhere, Woods sent for an undertaker and gave him his life insurance policy, asking the man to keep the premiums paid. He requested that when he was dead to embalm his body and lay it alongside his murdered wife near Yanceyville, North Carolina.

The *Times-Dispatch* reported, "He seemed resigned to his fate, and not worried."

64

Will Calloway

O N JULY 10, 1914, a Black Tennessee laborer named Will Calloway was executed in the electric chair at the unusual hour of 10:00 a.m. for the horrific cremation murder of his four-year-old nephew. He and his wife Lizzie had taken charge of the boy after the death of his mother. The murder occurred near Jonesville, in Lee County.

Evidence showed that Calloway, his wife, and little nephew, who lived "in a wild section of the Tennessee mountains," were traveling through Virginia into Kentucky when the weary child became fussy, irritating his uncle. With provisions low, the couple then decided the child was too great a burden and Calloway, according to his wife's version of the story, conceived the idea of murdering him.

After stopping near Jonesville for a rest, Calloway accumulated a large pile of brush and ignited it. When the fire was roaring, he grabbed the child, stripped away his clothes, and threw him into the flames.

Charred bones discovered by chance by passers-by, along with cryptic remarks uttered to locals by Lizzie led to an investigation by the Lee County authorities, and the arrest and conviction of the guilty pair.

Lizzie Calloway was guilty as an accessory to the horrendous crime but was spared electrocution by cooperating with the county authorities. She received 18 years in the State Penitentiary.

Calloway was a 38-year-old native of Knoxville, Tennessee, therefore his family directed E.B. Mann Undertaking on July 7 to inquire of the cost of "embalming the body, furnishing a cheap robe, and an A or B coffin," so Calloway's body could be prepared and shipped to Tennessee.

65

Willie Puryear

WILLIE PURYEAR, a Black 19-year-old Mecklenburg native, was convicted of criminal assault on a married mother of six children, then electrocuted August 7, 1914.

Almost immediately after sentencing, Puryear's sanity was questioned. "The stolid indifference exhibited by the negro to his fate after sentence, was pronounced," reported the *Richmond Times-Dispatch*. "His coolness and self-possession, and the fact that he suddenly became as silent as the sphynx, refusing to converse with anyone, created the impression in the minds of certain humane citizens that the condemned man was irresponsible for his actions at the time he committed the crime."

The *Washington Evening Star* expressed similar concern, stating that "there is a good deal of doubt as to whether the man really should go to the chair, though there is said to be no question of his guilt."

In deference to the wishes of numerous petitioners, Governor Stuart ordered a mental examination of Puryear "by competent authorities." Their report concluded there was "no reason to doubt [the prisoner's] sanity."

The governor thus declined to interfere with the death sentence.

66

Henry Coach

Nottoway County Black man Henry Coach, age 33, was executed at 7:07 a.m. on August 21, 1914, after being convicted of robbery and battery against 63-year-old Alexander Murdock, a White Nottoway County store owner and immigrant from Scotland.

Coach allegedly beat Murdock with a plow beam before robbing him of $60. Murdock died months later of angina pectoris and chronic nephritis. It is unknown if Coach's attack contributed to his death.

Coach was convicted and sentenced in Nottoway Circuit Court, and his conviction received a brief mention only in the *Blackstone Courier* newspaper.

67

John Edmunds

Twenty-seven-year-old Black Charlotte County native John Edmunds was electrocuted December 18, 1914, for the murder of Henry Morton, a 49-year-old Black man from Charlotte County. Edmunds was arrested after an all-day search in Prince Edward County.

Morton and a relative attended a circus in Farmville on October 9, and after leaving stopped about 15 miles down the road to talk to a mutual friend named Joe Lewis. During the conversation, Edmunds approached and suddenly shot Morton dead in front of several eyewitnesses. According to press accounts, Morton was well-liked, "and feelings among the people of Charlotte about the crime were intense."

It was also reported that Morton's body lay where it fell until early the next morning.

Edmunds, when arrested near his home, confessed to killing Morton but offered no reason for the shooting, although it was rumored to be over a woman. He went to the Prince Edward Jail, and a special term of the Prince Edward County Circuit Court was scheduled by Judge George J. Hundley to be held on October 22.

Law enforcement received a warning on October 11 that about 50 Prince Edward County citizens were organizing to overwhelm the jail, release and lynch Edmunds, a rare occurrence for a Black-on-Black crime. No one would accept the role of mob leader, however, so the plan was abandoned. Still, a squad of soldiers from the Farmville Guard and several deputized citizens guarded the jail "until excitement over the crime had abated."

1915

68

Arthur Neal

ON JANUARY 8, 1915, after being convicted in King William County of highway robbery and "attempt to commit rape upon Annie V__, a little Polish girl" described as "about 12 years old," Arthur Neale, a Black man, was executed in the electric chair. He was 18 years of age.

The alleged assault occurred October 2, 1914 near the town of West Point, between 4:00 and 5:00 p.m. A young employee at the pulp mills, V__ was on her way into town when Neal grabbed her. She began screaming, attracting the attention of several people nearby and frightening Neal away. The *Richmond Times-Dispatch* reported that "Several young men gave chase in automobiles, and he was caught about five miles from town and brought back."

He was taken to the girl, and she supposedly positively identified him. She was reported to be "bruised considerably and suffered from the nervous shock but otherwise was not injured."

Neal admitted attacking the girl but denied taking $5 from her, as she claimed.

Because of a delay in sending his record to the penitentiary after a last-minute attempt by his counsel to prevent his execution, Neale received one respite from the governor from his original execution date of December 11, 1914.

As possibly a result of the attack, the V__ family – who were immigrants from Croatia, not Poland – left West Point and by 1920 were living in Altoona, Washington.

69

Charles Miller

CHARLES MILLER, a Black man aged 29, died in the electric chair March 26, 1915, for the murder of John Fountain, another Black man, after a January 26 altercation in a South Boston pool hall.

On January 27, only 24 hours after the crime, Miller was tried, convicted of killing Fountain "in a drunken fight" and sentenced to death – an extraordinarily rapid turnaround for a Black-on-Back crime. Witnesses testified that the fight started when Fountain borrowed money from Miller and refused to pay it back.

Miller claimed he did not remember the fight, but the same eyewitnesses testified he stabbed Fountain through the heart.

On February 6, rumors of a possible lynching attempt forced authorities to transfer Miller from Halifax County to the Henrico County Jail for safekeeping. That same day, South Boston Sergeant E.N. Hardy received a message from Danville that the victim, Fountain, was wanted there for shooting a Black woman the previous Sunday.

Governor Stuart denied a request to commute Miller's sentence to life in the penitentiary.

70

Herbert Caple

HERBERT CAPLE, convicted of highway robbery in Sussex County, was executed on April 30, 1915.

In mid-February, the Black Caple hailed a "successful" White farmer from Story Creek named Joseph Fuller, asking for a ride on his horse-drawn wagon. While riding, he allegedly struck Fuller on the head with a rock or blunt instrument, "knocking him senseless." With the farmer down, Caple then robbed him of a small amount of cash.

Caple denied that he committed the crime, but Fuller "positively identified him as the assailant."

Judge J. F. West of the Sussex Circuit Court tried and sentenced Caple March 20. In the same session, Judge West also convicted a White man named William Peters of the similar crime of beating and maiming a Black man. Peters' punishment was not death, but a $20 fine.

After the trial, Caple had to be transferred to the Petersburg Jail for safekeeping because of lynching rumors.

The execution of the 24-year-old "negro highwayman" was the first for highway robbery in Sussex County in over 50 years, and one of only a few non-homicide executions reserved only for Black men.

When Caple's family could not afford to transport his body back to Sussex for burial, it by law was claimed by the State Anatomical Board and sent to the dissecting room of the Medical College of Virginia.

71

Skipwith Sydnor

SKIPWITH SYDNOR, a Black farmer from Halifax County, was executed May 21, 1915, in the electric chair for murdering a man described by some press outlets as being his brother, Charles Saddle, on April 19, 1914.

After a heated argument over an unknown household issue, Skipwith, age 24 or 25, reportedly slashed Saddle numerous times with a straight razor.

Saddle may have been a stepbrother or maybe no relation at all. He was listed in a court document as being 80 years old, and an 1890 census record for Sydnor's family contains no one by that name.

There were no petitions for clemency or stays of executions filed. The entire press coverage of this case was five lines in the May 19, 1915, *Richmond Times-Dispatch* announcing the electrocution.

72

Thomas Cole

TWENTY-TWO-YEAR-OLD Boydton native Thomas Cole, also known as Tom Cole, was electrocuted at 7:20 a.m. on June 4, 1915.

The Mecklenburg County Circuit Court found Cole, a Black laborer, guilty of "indecent assault" (rape or attempted rape) against a 15-year-old White girl from Buffalo Junction. He was also indicted for the January 31 handgun murder of a Black Mecklenburg woman named Babe Chandler in a "crime of passion." After being sentenced to death in the Royster assault he did not stand trial for the Chandler crime. He received the death penalty for raping a White woman but not for killing a Black woman.

There were no respites or appeals. The Anatomical Board at the Medical College claimed his body.

The White victim died in Montgomery, Alabama in January 1988.

73

Lemuel "Lem" Jones

FOR THE FIRST TIME in many years, an execution took place at the Virginia Penitentiary on a day other than Friday, when Lem Jones, *alias* "Blind Man," a 19-year-old Black Norfolk resident, was electrocuted Thursday, June 10, 1915. The Corporation Court of Norfolk convicted and sentenced Jones to die for the murder of Isaac Aleck, a White merchant, in his store on Washington Avenue.

His execution was a result of grossly inadequate legal representation, coupled with a most likely case of mistaken identity.

Around midnight on September 15, 1914, Aleck and his wife were closing for the night when Jones, Luke Dozier, and Dave McDonald entered the store. As Aleck's wife watched in horror from around a corner, one of the men drew a revolver and ordered Aleck to put up his hands, but Aleck grabbed a meat cleaver that was lying on the counter and as he was about to attack, he was shot in the chest. The men fled empty-handed.

Jones and Dozier were quickly captured but McDonald escaped to North Carolina. Dozier turned him in, however, and he was arrested when he returned to Norfolk a week later.

One of several problems with this case is that Aleck's wife in a line-up positively identified a fourth Black man named Howard as the one who shot her husband. Howard, however, proved he was nowhere near the crime scene. With Howard ruled out, Mrs. Aleck then identified Jones as the murderer. Jones, on the other hand, insisted it was McDonald who pulled the trigger against Aleck.

Jones testified at McDonald and Dozier's trials that he had conspired with them to rob the store, but that McDonald unexpectedly shot Aleck when he approached with the cleaver. Dozier also testified during his trial that McDonald, not Jones, was the triggerman. Dozier and McDonald both received life sentences in the penitentiary

McDonald, however, testified for the prosecution against Dozier and Jones. For turning State's evidence, he was rewarded by having his penitentiary term reduced from life to 18 years.

Despite the confusion of who shot the storekeeper Aleck, Jones, represented by two young attorneys trying their very first case, received a death sentence.

WELL-KNOWN PEOPLE ASK CLEMENCY FOR NEGRO

Petition Governor to Commute Sentence of Lem Jones, Convicted of Murder.

City officials and "several prominent citizens" strongly suspected eyewitness misidentification, resulting in an unfair trial for Jones. On May 11 they applied to commute Jones's sentence from death to life imprisonment, reminding Governor Stuart that Aleck's widow was just as positive when she identified an innocent man as the murderer as when she identified Jones. Also, Jones was defended by two young lawyers who had never tried a single case, much less a death penalty case.

Governor Stuart refused the application, and the execution proceeded.

74

Luther Canter

L UTHER CANTER was the first White man in two years to die in the electric chair when he was electrocuted June 19, 1915, for the assault and murder of 20-year-old Maude Wilson, also White, near the Bristol-Abingdon Turnpike the previous April 24.

Maude, the wife of James R. Wilson, a well-known Washington County farmer, was murdered while preparing to leave the house to spend the night with her in-laws while her husband was out of town helping with farm work. Canter entered the house then gagged and bound Wilson's hands with strips of cloth, tying her to the bedpost. After allegedly raping her, Canter stabbed her in the breast with a large knife. Finding a shotgun over the door, he then shot her in the abdomen.

Wilson's father-in-law, Edward Wilson, found her body later that night when she never showed up. She was reportedly lying in a pool of blood, nearly nude, her hands still tied to the bedpost.

In a sad irony, the shotgun was left loaded in the bedroom by Maude's husband for her protection in his absence.

Sheriff J. A. Miller and the Bristol police began a full investigation. A police officer found the shotgun about 300 yards away near the home of John Canter and his two sons, 24-year-old Luther, who was not home, and 21-year-old James, or Jimmie. Jimmie was arrested as a suspect and sent to prison at Abingdon to await trial.

Finding out that his brother had been arrested, Luther, who reportedly "had a bad reputation" among the locals, admitted to his neighbor R. F. Preston and two brothers named Legard that he committed the murder, and was scared he would be lynched.

Preston and the Legards then took Luther to Abingdon and surrendered him to Sheriff Miller. Persistent rumors of a lynch mob forming, however, forced Miller to take him on the evening passenger train to the Roanoke Jail for safekeeping.

At Luther's May 6 arraignment, he pled guilty and confessed the entire crime. With a jury trial unnecessary, and after the court heard from witnesses and examined the evidence, he was found guilty of first-degree murder and sentenced to death. He was then ordered back to jail for the night to await his brother's trial the next day.

An overflow crowd packed the Abingdon courtroom on May 7 to witness Jimmie Canter's trial of being an accomplice of his brother in the rape and murder of Maude Wilson. While Jimmie was allegedly completely innocent, he was unfortunately a disaster on the stand, continually making misstatements, stumbling, and contradicting himself. He even at one point admitted to assaulting the woman under pointed questioning from the prosecutor.

His case was also hurt by a prosecution witness, Mary Worley, who stated that on two occasions Jimmie had made "lewd conversation, indicating his lecherous disposition and lustful desires toward Mrs. Wilson."

But after Luther took the stand, the *Richmond Times-Dispatch* claimed the crowd "found themselves in a fever of excitement soon after Luther, condemned the previous day to die for the crime, began to tell the harrowing story of the assault and murder."

> He stated the horrible details of how he entered Mrs. Wilson's room at their home and finding her there alone, seized her and after a fierce struggle finally

overcame, bound and attacked her ... He denied Jimmie had anything to do with the crime, and that he acted alone.

During Luther Canter's testimony, the crowd became loud and hostile. Fearing an open revolt, Judge Preston Campbell ordered the courtroom cleared. He immediately adjourned and ordered the Canter brothers hustled under armed guard to a nearby Norfolk & Western Railway station. Luther was sent to Roanoke and Jimmie to Marion.

Despite Luther's continued claims that his brother was innocent, prosecutor N.P. Oglesby was absolutely convinced that Jimmie was with Luther, and was equally guilty. The jury agreed, and at sentencing on May 8, both Luther and Jimmie Canter were sentenced to die in the electric chair.

On May 13, less than a month before his execution, Jimmie received a writ of error from the Supreme Court of Virginia, delaying his execution. The decision followed a visit to Oglesby's office by John Canter, father of the condemned brothers, who insisted that Jimmie was with him the day of the murder. After pleading with the attorney to save his younger son, a "pathetic appeal" also came from Jimmie in the Roanoke City Jail.

The appeals changed Oglesby's mind. "Although he is illiterate and may never amount to much in human society, that is not the issue," he wrote of Jimmie in an appeal to the governor. "The Lord put him here for some reason, and if he is not guilty, he has the same right to live that I have." Oglesby entered no plea to save Luther, however.

It was up to the governor to save Jimmie's life.

On June 19, five minutes before he went to the chair, Luther confessed to his spiritual adviser, Rev. Samuel H. Templeton, that Jimmie again was innocent and had nothing to do with the murder. That confession, along with the appeals from Oglesby and the family, convinced the governor, but instead of releasing Jimmie he instead just commuted his death sentence to life imprisonment, despite the fact it was never proven at trial he was ever at the scene of the crime, other than his blurted admittance under duress.

As a fortuitous postscript, Jimmie did not serve his entire life sentence in the penitentiary. His attorney went to work to reverse his conviction, and finally, after an astonishing five more trials, he was acquitted and had all charges reversed in a 1918 Virginia Supreme Court case, Canter v. Commonwealth.

Jimmie Canter died in Abingdon on May 30, 1971, at age 73.

75

George Matthews

76

John Rollins

ON AUGUST 20, 1915, George Matthews, *alias* George Rollins, was electrocuted moments before his cousin, John Lewis Rollins after both were convicted of raping Burnleigh Coleman and attempting to rape her daughter, Eula Coleman, at their cottage near Bowling Green in western Caroline County.

Both Black men were natives of Caroline, but John Rollins had recently returned after living in Jersey City for eleven years. Constable Tom Boulware arrested them, and in yet another case of "swift justice," went to trial only four days later.

On July 15 Rollins openly confessed to attacking the Coleman girl. He then implicated Matthews and waived trial by jury. The court convened at 10:30 a.m. for Matthews, and a grand jury brought indictments against each of the prisoners. Judge Chichester advised the jury to "consider each detail of the evidence presented most carefully so that there might be no suspicion of prejudice or vengeance in their decision."

W.E. Ennis, assisted by Colonel Richard L. Beale represented the Commonwealth, but Matthews and Rollins had no defense counsel because all attorneys who were not engaged in other cases had left town for summer vacations.

During the trial, the men turned against one another, with Matthews confessing that Rollins was the ringleader. Rollins similarly claimed in his confession that Mathews instigated the attacks.

The two Coleman women lived in Washington D. C. but came to their former home in Bowling Green because Eula suffered from nervous exhaustion, and her mother thought the "native air of their old home" would be rejuvenating. They were alone in the house on the morning of July 11, when Eula awakened. As reported by the July 15, 1915, *Washington Evening Star*, "Seeing the woolly, kinky hair of John Lewis Rollins, she thought it was a dog and called to her mother, 'There's a dog in my room.' The mother, who was being attacked in the next bedroom, then heard Eula call back, 'There's a negro in my room.'"

Described as "desperately weak from her terrible ordeal with Matthews" but overwhelmed with fear for the safety of her daughter, Coleman tore herself away and ran to her daughter's rescue, preventing her rape.

Fighting for their lives, the women drove the two men from the house and barricaded the doors and windows. Undeterred, Rollins and Matthews attempted three times to reach a second-story window with a ladder, but each time the women pushed it over as the men tried to climb up. One of the men at one point even tried to carry a hatchet with him.

The yells of the women alerted a neighbor, finally scaring away Matthews and Rollins. A policeman offered his opinion on the stand that the men intended to kill the women and set fire to the house to hide their crime.

Angry local townspeople arrived by car and horse from all over Caroline for the trial, but there were no credible threats of lynching and no disruptions in the courtroom.

The press reported the jury pronounced them guilty and imposed the death penalty after less than five minutes of deliberation. A news account stated that "a few of the colored woman relatives of the prisoners made an outcry [at the jury's verdict], but overall the courtroom was quiet, crowded with persons both colored and white."

Erring on the side of caution, on July 16 Richmond Sheriff T. B. Gill took both men to the Henrico County Jail for safekeeping until they were transported to the penitentiary for execution.

77

Edward Proyor

CONVICTED AND SENTENCED to death twice in Surry County for highway robbery, 30-year-old Black laborer Edward Proyor (also spelled Pryor by the penitentiary and in newspaper accounts) was electrocuted September 10, 1915. A motion for a third trial was overruled.

On September 29, 1914, Proyor allegedly severely beat a 16-year-old White teenager named Cecil Clyde Pittman, robbing him of about $11 in silver coins.

After being convicted and sentenced to death in Surry County Circuit Court, Proyor appealed that his sentence was unjustly harsh. Judge Jesse F. West granted a new trial, but he again was sentenced to death.

While in the Richmond city jail for safekeeping, Proyor deluged Governor Stuart with special delivery messages, telegrams, and even verbal pleas via friends begging for executive clemency. When the governor went to San Francisco in July, Proyor feared he would not return in time to give his case his full attention. Then, on July 25, after reading in the newspaper that the governor had arrived back in Richmond, he sent him a letter marked "personal:"

> I heerd you was back. That awful day is fast approaching, and you must do something to save me. I was convicted on secenstanum evidence entirely and that illegal, as you probably know. I don't see how you can resist my plea in view of the much interest in this community about my case. I is an innocent man and didn't get a fair trial.
>
> (signed)
> Ed Proyor

Proyor stated in this and other letters that he was not looking to be released, but would even be satisfied if the governor commuted his sentence to life imprisonment. "Anything but that thar chair," he wrote.

Governor Stuart considered the merits of Proyor's plea with Judge West, who presided at both Surry trials. He "found nothing to change his mind," so the execution proceeded.

Suffering no permanent injuries from the attack, Pittman moved on with his life, later working as a machine operator at a Hercules plant near Hopewell. He died in 1967, at 69 years of age.

78

Sherman Stanfield

EIGHTEEN-YEAR-OLD Black Pittsylvania farm laborer Sherman Stanfield was executed on September 17, 1915, at 7:10 a.m. for "felonious assault with intent to commit rape" on a 5-year-old White Danville girl.

Stanfield was apprehended three days after the June 3 attack by a Mountain Hill farmer named G. C. Chaney. Chaney somehow subdued Stanfield and delivered him 10 miles to authorities in Danville. Based on the eyewitness identification of the victim, the Pittsylvania County Circuit Court convicted and sentenced him to die.

At the time of the attack, Stanfield had been married a little over a year to Hester Oliver Stanfield.

1916

79

Percy Ellis

THE YOUNGEST PERSON ever executed in Virginia's electric chair, 16-year-old Percy Ellis, died at 7:15 a.m. on March 15, 1916, for murder in the city of Norfolk. He was the youngest person executed since 1787 when the slave Clem was hanged in Richmond at the age of 12.

Ellis was charged with the September 23, 1915 shooting of 37-year-old Nathan Cohen, a White Norfolk storekeeper. Cohen reprimanded Ellis after creating a disturbance in front of his store at Oberndorfer Road during business hours, provoking Ellis to pull out a pistol and shoot him in the abdomen. Cohen died on September 27 at St. Vincent's Hospital after developing gangrene.

After his February 5 trial in the Corporation Court of Norfolk, counsel moved for a new trial, but it was overruled and the defendant accepted the ruling.

Frontpage coverage of Ellis' execution focused not on the defendant's age but on the reasons he died on a Wednesday rather than the traditional Friday. The penitentiary superintendent insisted that Fridays alone were never reserved for executions, and there was no particular reason why Ellis died on a Wednesday.

His body, like many, was sent to the Medical College Anatomical Board for dissection.

80

Joseph Lee

JOE LEE, a Black Caroline County resident charged with the November 6, 1915 murder of Frank Grymes, also Black, near Rappahannock Academy, was executed on April 21, 1916.

Supposedly at the behest of Gryme's wife, Carrie, Lee went to their house at 3:00 a.m. and knocked on the door. When Grymes answered, Lee shot him, killing him instantly. He then dragged the body into the nearby woods, piled brush over it, lit it on fire, and kept it burning for two days.

The prosecution claimed at the trial that Grymes' wife furnished Lee with coal oil to burn the body. Lee had attempted to cover up the immolation by spreading the ashes, but small bones and teeth were found at the location and exhibited to the jury. Lee did not take the stand, and he had no defense witnesses.

The jury was out one hour and came back with a verdict of first-degree murder and a recommended sentence of death. Judge Chichester did not pronounce sentence right away, as Lee was to be a witness in Carrie Grymes' trial after she was charged with being an accessory to the murder.

On December 24, Carrie Grymes was found guilty of being an accessory in the murder of her husband and sentenced to 10 years in the penitentiary.

Of particular interest is Joe Lee's age. He repeatedly claimed in his trial to be 83 years of age, but the court had reason to believe he was more realistically 68. A Caroline County marriage record from 1870 shows a Joseph L. Lee born near Bowling Green in 1848, confirming his age at 68. Lee may have claimed the older age to elicit sympathy from the court to avoid execution.

Whether 83 or 68, he is still the oldest prisoner executed in Virginia's electric chair, and his execution coincidentally followed the youngest prisoner to be executed by electrocution, Percy Ellis.

81

John Williams

JOHN HENRY WILLIAMS, age 23, died in the electric chair on May 26, 1916, for the crime of assault at gunpoint on March 29 against 19-year-old White Nottoway woman Mamie Mason. The crime occurred near Blackstone.

Williams allegedly attacked his schoolgirl victim while she, her younger brother Marshall and sister Anna walked on a lonely country road. Upon his quick arrest, the county exploded as the news of the attack spread, and according to the May 27 *Richmond Times-Dispatch*, locals "became so aroused by the crime that the governor's office was almost to the point of calling out the militia to restore quiet."

On April 2, an estimated 1,000 "enraged citizens" from Nottoway and Dinwiddie Counties surrounded the Petersburg Jail, where Williams was temporarily held. Reportedly "shaking in terror" while the mob stoned the jail, Williams "begged piteously for protection" before allegedly confessing to attacking the Mason woman.

"Lynching was in the air," the *Alexandria Gazette* reported, "and the presence of a determined leader might have resulted in violence."

Petersburg Mayor Cabaniss dispersed the mob by declaring citywide martial law, but at midnight there was still such unrest that he called Henrico County Sheriff W. Sydnor for assistance. Sydnor – accompanied by a group of armed Richmond deputies – drove to Petersburg in an automobile and "spirited the negro on back roads to the Henrico Jail."

The incident generated so much publicity that it forced an anti-lynching editorial in the April 4, 1916 *Gazette*:

> In the Commonwealth there is no excuse for lynchings, for the administration of the law in such cases is swift and impartial. When guilt is proved, punishment is certain. To supplant the orderly procedure of courts of justice with the mad vengeance and utter ferocity of a mob is for our people themselves to descend to the level of the brute.

While jailed in Henrico, Mason's brother and sister positively identified Williams from a lineup.

A huge crowd of onlookers showed up at the April 21 trial in Nottoway, with people even crowding the windows. Deputies resorted to searching everyone entering for concealed weapons, and one man, when found to have a hidden pistol, was quickly arrested. The *Richmond Times-Dispatch* reported that at the trial, "Only a few negroes were present, having been warned to stay away."

One of the witnesses was an elderly Black man named Jim Cook, who lived only a few hundred yards from where the attack took place. Williams had spent the night with Cook and had even borrowed his gun to use in the attack the next day. Cook was asked when he took the stand if he could identify the assailant. He pointed at Williams and reportedly exclaimed, "Yes, dar [sic] he is."

Then, according to the *Times-Dispatch*. he surprised the court by admonishing the defendant, even after the judge ordered him to stop. "You are a mean nigger; you lied to me; you told me you was a good man and a member of the church and you would do nothing wrong."

The reporter was impressed by the outburst. "The honesty and the straightforwardness of the old darky made of him one of the best witnesses and impressed all with his sincerity."

After several Black men were summoned to sit on either side of Williams, the victim's siblings entered to see if they could identify their sister's assailant. The prosecutor then asked the 12-year-old boy, Marshall, if he could point to the man who attacked his sister. He reportedly walked right up to Williams, poked his finger on his forehead, and exclaimed "This is the one."

Williams "seemed to shudder at that moment."

"A murmur of satisfaction ran through the courtroom when this scene was enacted."

Williams later nervously took the stand but in a composed voice made an articulate and impassioned plea that he be allowed to live and make amends for his crime, which he claimed was due to alcoholism. "You have the power to show mercy to me as you hope to have it shown to you," he implored, "and in this tumult of white people I wish to say that it is my desire to live a Christian life in the future, and am willing to spend my days in confinement so that I may die a natural death."

But it was all for nothing. After 13 minutes of deliberation, the jury returned with a verdict of guilty and a sentence of death. Judge Southall claimed it was not in his power to change the verdict, and would not even do so if he could. The commonwealth's attorney congratulated the courtroom spectators for their orderliness during this "trying ordeal."

After conviction, Williams returned by train back to the Henrico County Jail. While there he feigned violent insanity, and at one point it appeared that the execution would have to be stayed "until he returned to normal mind." Once he was removed to the penitentiary, however, he seemed to be resigned to his fate and reportedly on the day of execution went quietly to the chamber.

After the execution, Governor Stuart sent a letter of thanks to Henrico Sheriff Sydnor for his assistance in the case.

82

Milton Mallory

BLACK 19-YEAR-OLD Wise County hotel porter and reputed serial rapist Milton Mallory (also spelled Malloy and Maloy) was executed in the State Penitentiary on July 7, 1916. The Circuit Court of Wise County on June 22 refused his writ of innocence.

Mallory was accused of raping six young girls between the ages of 5 and 11 over 8 weeks ending May 13, 1916. He was executed for the May 1 rape of a 9-year-old, his only apparent White victim. She was one of four daughters of a local bank president, and an immigrant from Great Britain. According to the prosecution, Mallory gave his victims candy containing a sedative, then attacked them.

Before his May 16 trial, Mallory had to be sequestered deep in the mountains near Appalachia to prevent mob violence. At the beginning of his trial in Wise County Court, Judge Skeen announced he was ordering a search for weapons, and if anyone had a weapon to leave the courtroom at once. The *Alexandria Gazette* reported fifteen men got up and left.

In a letter dated July 1 to State Penitentiary Superintendent Wood, Mallory's attorneys stated that "Milton Mallory's mother, an elegant type of colored woman, wants to know what is necessary for her to do, to get the body of her son." Wood replied that A. D. Price, a Black undertaker on Leigh Street in Richmond, would embalm the body, furnish a coffin or box and ship it to Norton or Appalachia for $50.00. "The express on the body alone will cost $20.00, as they generally charge twice as much for a dead body as they do a live person."

The mother elected to not bring her son's body back to Wise so as not to "have it exposed to a curious crowd." He instead went to the Medical College dissecting room.

83

Clifford Mickens

ON AUGUST 25, 1916, 19-year-old Black Roanoke cook Clifford Mickens went to the electric chair for the slaying of White police officer J. Harvey Leverett, age 22.

Mickens was charged on three counts – felonious murder, feloniously attempting to commit robbery by violence, and felonious robbery from the person. Roanoke business owners George Dyer and J.W. Wills also identified Mickens as the man who robbed them on separate occasions at their places of business.

Mickens was described as short and heavy-set, about 5 feet 2 inches and weighing about 146 pounds. When questioned about the killing of Officer Leverett, the *Roanoke World News* reported he "displayed remarkable indifference."

On August 8, as State Penitentiary Officers Penn and Hall arrived to escort Mickens to Richmond, Mickens' brother Herman, who had testified against him, arrived to say goodbye. Mickens – bound hand and foot by steel shackles – only told his brother "Tell mama goodbye for me."

While at the train station, Mickens told a *Roanoke World News* reporter that "If I could write the Governor a letter, and make him see it the way I does, I would."

Mickens' mother, Virginia Mickens of High Street in Roanoke, wrote a letter to Superintendent Wood asking how to take possession of her son's body. On August 14, Wood replied that she needed to contact A. D. Price, the Richmond undertaker, who "usually looks after these things for the friends of any condemned men."

She worked out an arrangement, as Mickens' body after the execution was shipped to Troutville for burial.

84

Richard Green

A 19-YEAR-OLD Black part-time fireman named Richard Green immediately followed Clifford Mickens to the electric chair at 7:20 a.m. on August 25, 1916. Green was convicted of murder in Charlotte County.

Details are scarce, but what is known is that on June 24, a drunk and disorderly Green was asked to leave a Whites-only soda fountain. Refusing to go, he was later physically removed by one of the owners.

Enraged by this embarrassment, Green returned later with a pistol and started shooting indiscriminately, killing 11-year-old Gabriel Jones and wounding several others.

85

Henry Lewis

HENRY LEWIS, Black, age 23, died in the electric chair on September 8, 1916, for the stabbing murder of Mary Willie Crawford, also Black, on May 15. A jury convicted Lewis in the Corporation Court of Lynchburg on June 7. A motion for a new trial was dismissed.

He admitted to being a drug addict but denied killing anyone.

86

James Corbett

JAMES CORBETT, a 22-year-old Black man, was executed on October 2, 1916, for murder. He was convicted in the Corporation Court of Norfolk.

Almost nothing is known of this case. Corbett's original execution date was September 15, but a respite had to be granted on September 14 because of a delay in getting the receipt of conviction to the penitentiary on time. The delay made it impossible to comply with the law that stipulated the prisoner must be confined there no less than 15 days before execution.

87

Mincie Harris

MINCIE HARRIS, a 19-year-old Black native of Buckingham County, followed James Corbett to the electric chair on October 2, 1916. Harris was convicted of the "assault and robbery" of Bennett Branch, described as an "aged white woman" living at Warminster.

According to the *Alexandria Gazette*, Harris went to Branch's house in early May and demanded to know where she hid her money. When she refused to tell him, Harris allegedly slashed her throat with a knife and fled empty-handed.

A neighbor later discovered Branch and despite her wound was able to describe her attacker. Police later arrested Harris as he tried to board a train.

While rape was not mentioned in any of the scarce news accounts, the 1916 *Journal of the Virginia House of Delegates* states that Harris was convicted of rape and was originally sentenced to die on July 14. He received numerous respites due to possible misidentification by the victim.

1917

88

Hansom Warren

ON JUNE 15, 1917, a 23-year-old Black Isle of Wight tenant laborer named Hansom Warren went to the electric chair for the ax murder of prominent Day's Point farmer Thomas J. Seward.

Warren was a tenant on Seward's farm, and on January 30 Seward walked to Warren's house to inquire why he did not come to work. Warren replied that "he must be notified overnight" if he was needed for work the next day.

Seward reportedly replied "That is no way to act," then turned and walked away. Warren then allegedly picked up a nearby ax and struck Seward in the hack of his head, "cleaving it almost in two," according to the *Newport News Daily Press*.

A neighbor spotted the mortally wounded Seward outside Warren's house and called Dr. L. C. Brock and Sheriff Edwards. Meanwhile, after taking money from Seward, Warren tried to get away in Seward's rowboat.

A telephone network assembled about 40 citizens, and three men named Bloxom, Carter, and Jordan caught Warren as he tried to cross the James River near Battery Park. He was then taken to jail in Smithfield.

Despite his gruesome injuries, Seward clung to life for nine agonizing days until he died February 9 at 10:00 a.m. He was reportedly a well-liked farmer, 35 years of age, with a wife, Eleanor, and two young sons, Thomas and Charles Wesley.

During the trial in early May, there were rumors of mob violence but it never amounted to more than angry words. Judge B. D. White sentenced Warren to death in the Isle of Wight County Court.

89

Robert Jones

90

Hamilton Cosby

ROBERT JONES and Hamilton Cosby, two Black men convicted on April 19, 1917, by a jury in the Charlottesville Corporation Court for the murder of Charlottesville Policeman Meredith A. Thomas, died in the electric chair within minutes of each other on June 20. Thomas caught them in the act of stealing hams from a store in Charlottesville, and a shoot-out resulted in his murder.

After the arrest of the culprits on April 16, an angry mob descended on the Charlottesville jail and for three hours besieged it, trying to get to the two prisoners. Soon the crowd became so large and unruly it became impossible for Monticello Guards and Charlottesville firemen to control them.

Suddenly, Judge A. D. Dabney of the Corporation Court arrived and faced down the gale-force mob at the jail entrance. He formally opened court at 1:00 a.m. then ordered the unlawful assemblage to disperse. The huge crowd of men, many masked in handkerchiefs, reluctantly backed away from the jail and went home.

On April 18, the Charlottesville courtroom was jammed with agitated White and Black spectators, watched over by a contingent of National Guardsmen. No one attempted to start a protest. Jones and Cosby both pleaded not guilty.

In sentencing, Judge Dabney claimed that "at no time were [the defendants] in danger of mob violence," and he asserted that the presence of the armed militia was unnecessary.

After the execution, Cosby's grandfather, Richard Cosby, of Charlottesville, requested his grandson's body. "The Grand-father is a very respectable colored man of this county," Cosby's lawyer Albert Bolling wrote on May 8, 1917, to Penitentiary Superintendent Wood, "who has the regard of the white citizens here."

91

Albert Barrett

ALBERT BARRETT, a 35-year-old Black Charlotte County man, died in the electric chair on August 31, 1917, for the murder of prominent county farmer W. T. Roach. Roach's mangled body, with his head badly crushed, was found July 17 hidden in a thicket near his home near the town of Red House, about 12 miles south of Appomatox.

On July 16 Roach suspected Barrett and his 14-year-old son Aubrey of stealing wheat from his barn, so he and a friend went to the Barrett home to confront the elder Barrett about the theft. Roach sent his friend for a warrant while he remained as a guard until the official paper could be served. While his friend was gone, the *Richmond Planet* reported that Barrett offered to pay for the wheat rather than go to court, but when Roach refused, Barrett murdered him after a short pursuit on foot.

The Barretts hid the body then disappeared for two days, but they were immediately suspected when someone discovered Roach's decomposed body. A lynch mob quickly formed, and on July 19 a mass of almost 250 men captured the Barretts at Mt. Zion, in Campbell County, about 15 miles from the scene of the crime. The Barrett's reportedly confessed the murder to the mob, who immediately started with them back to Red House.

It was reported at the town of Gladys that the mob was returning to Red House to lynch the entire Barrett family, including not just Albert and Aubrey, but Albert's wife, Mattie, son Albert Jr. and daughters Lola and Mary. A lack of telephone communication made it difficult for anyone to get reliable information, as the mob intentionally cut the trunk line in their search for the Barretts.

Meanwhile, 10 Baldwin-Felts detectives, hearing that the mob was returning the Barretts to Red House, left on a train from Roanoke, hoping to reach Red House before the mob returned and a lynching occurred. They arrived at Gladys at 3:00 a.m. and hearing the mob was at Mt. Zion, set out in automobiles but were turned back by roads made impassable by recent heavy rains. While in Gladys, they heard that several hundred men had passed through town earlier. One merchant claimed a half-dozen persons awakened him wanting to buy gasoline to set the six members of the Barrett family on fire.

Governor Henry Stuart sent orders to Lt. Colonel Robert Craighill to assemble the Lynchburg Home Guard for immediate mob duty after it was learned that the angry crowd had Albert Barrett and his son surrounded near Winfall, a small station on the L&D railroad, 17 miles south of Lynchburg. Stuart's orders were to assemble Company E and hold the command in readiness to move on notice. Fearing that the sounding of the military alarm "99" on the courthouse bell would cause undue panic in the city, the governor instead phoned Craighill with the orders at 8:45 a.m. By 9:30, more than 80 guardsmen were at the Lynchburg armory in uniform, ready for duty.

Later that morning three members of a sheriff's posse came across five men with Aubrey Barrett in an automobile stalled in deep mud. They took charge of Barrett without incident.

Meanwhile, a crowd of armed men gathered in a field to debate the fate of Albert Barrett when Campbell County Sheriff R. L. Perrow and Charlotte County Sheriff J. C. Priddy finally reached Red House. The mob had swelled to over 500, all angrily arguing among themselves whether the elder Barrett should be soaked in gasoline and lit on fire, shot, or hanged.

Their attitudes cooled, however, after Sheriff Perrow, Commonwealth Attorney A. H. Light and others appealed to them to forget lynching and let the law take its course. They eventually agreed and law enforcement took charge of a relieved Barrett. He and Aubrey reunited in the Lynchburg Jail.

On July 27 at 10:00 a.m. a special term of the court convened for five hours for the Barretts' hearing. Several hundred persons reportedly attended, with no trouble.

Because he was a juvenile, Aubrey was tried by Judge George J. Hundley, who pronounced him guilty after reviewing the evidence entered against him.

During Albert's trial, ten witnesses testified, including Barrett's daughter, Lola, who stated that Roach attacked her father first. The commonwealth's attorney surprisingly concurred that Roach had indeed attacked Albert Barrett first, throwing the prosecution into confusion. Both Barretts still confessed their crime, however; the younger Aubrey testified that he struck Roach on the head as he attacked his father, and then claimed that his father beat Roach on the head with a chunk of wood.

Regardless of the confusing testimony and claims of self-defense, Albert Barrett received a death sentence.

An important distinction was raised during Aubrey's sentencing. He had been represented to the court as being 14 years of age, but after evidence proved he was 17, Judge Hundley also sentenced him to death.

On August 30, the day before the scheduled executions, an outcry regarding the fairness of the trials forced Governor Stuart to grant a 30-day respite to Aubrey Barrett to examine the age discrepancies and because no lawyer was present when the judge sentenced him to death. Counsel for the elder Barrett quickly appealed his death sentence to the Virginia Supreme Court since testimony proved he was not only acting in self-defense, but that premeditation was not proven – both necessary for a first-degree murder conviction.

Judge Hundley, a Confederate veteran regarded as one of the "most distinguished men in Virginia," who sentenced both Albert and Aubrey Barrett to death, was furious about being second-guessed in the Barrett cases. He vigorously defended the trial and his actions, stating that attacks by newspapers, critics, and even State Senator Walter E. Addison "undermine and discredit the authority of the courts."

"Any ignoramus or crank can at his will besmirch the reputation of any judge," Hundley blustered, "and have the newspapers spread his slanders broadcast over the State."

Four of the five members of the Supreme Court refused to grant a writ of error in the case of Albert Barrett, and all efforts to commute his execution failed.

Exasperated by the criticism the case continued to generate, Judge Hundley penned a letter to the *Richmond Times-Dispatch* in hopes of ending the controversy:

> Sir, in regard to the Barrett case, this will be my last
> say on that matter. Some people seem determined to

try that case over again in the newspapers. Let that trial proceed. I never try cases in the newspapers. The court trial, with its records, is behind me. For the integrity of my action, I am responsible only to God ... The Governor, whom I respect and admire, knows that I asked him to keep troops in readiness for my call, to protect that very boy from mob violence, in case, after I heard the evidence, I should think he ought not to be sentenced to death. He knows I told him I would not be dictated to by any mob ...

While Albert Barrett's execution proceeded as planned on August 31, his son Aubrey's death sentence remained problematic. Since he did not receive a trial by jury because of the judge's mistaken belief he was only 14 years of age, he had no lawyer. In September, State Senator Walter Addison of Lynchburg appealed to Governor Stuart on behalf of the young man, and the case was appealed to the Supreme Court. But because there was no original trial there was no record, thus the appellate court found nothing upon which to base an opinion.

Following this action, several people interested in saving Aubrey's life sought executive clemency. Finally, after several respites, on November 16, 1917, Governor Stuart commuted Aubrey Barrett's sentence to life in prison.

Aubrey did not spend his life in prison. While he was still listed as a penitentiary inmate in 1920, a 1930 census record shows he had been released sometime the previous decade, and he and his younger brother, Albert Jr., had moved in with their aunt Lola Jones in New York City, where Aubrey was working as a truck driver. By 1940 he was married to a woman named Elnora and they had a son, Harvey.

1918

92

William Burgess

ILLIAM H. BURGESS, 32 years old of Halls Hill in Fairfax County, and a Black man described by the *Alexandria Gazette* as "towering over six feet, possessing great muscular power and having a rather vicious face," was executed January 26, 1918, for attempted assault on two White women, Mildred Miller and Mary Davis, in Alexandria County on or around August 23, 1917.

The press reported that Burgess's first attack occurred at Miller's home on Friday afternoon. She was alone when he purportedly entered, grabbed her, and struck her in the mouth, lacerating her lip and knocking out two of her teeth. Wrenching herself free, she screamed for help, and Burgess fled when he saw a vehicle approaching.

Fairfax Sheriff Allison claimed that it appeared that the attempted attack on Miss Davis occurred while Burgess fled the Miller home. He testified that when he arrived, she was unconscious "from the shock of the attack."

Armed with a description, the search for Burgess began immediately. Bloodhounds arrived from Occoquan workhouse, and they picked up Burgess's trail and followed it to his hiding place. When driven from cover, he ran and a Sheriff's Deputy shot at him, striking his hand.

Burgess had a wife and two children at Halls Hill. He supposedly went to work for the Southern Railway near Fairfax the previous Wednesday, but a supervisor reported that he worked two days then disappeared without asking for his pay. The attacks on the women occurred soon after he left his job.

After his arrest on August 25, Governor Stuart ordered Burgess moved for safekeeping after Fairfax's Sheriff Allison and Sheriff Fields of Alexandria told him by phone that a lynch mob was quickly forming there.

"There will be no lynching in Virginia in this instance," the governor proclaimed before ordering the prisoner to Richmond. Sheriff Allison arrived with Burgess on the 9:50 train that night and escorted the prisoner to the Henrico County Jail. Burgess's right hand was heavily bandaged from the shot through his palm.

Sheriff Allison admitted that Fairfax and Alexandria citizens were enraged by Burgess' alleged crimes, but he was so determined to adhere to Governor Stuart's strict demands to safeguard the prisoner that he ordered a squad of fifty soldiers to escort them to the train.

While transferring Burgess from the train station to the Henrico County Sheriff's automobile, Allison told Sheriff Sydnor and Henrico County Police Chief T. Wilson that Burgess confessed on the train his attempt to attack the women. Allison also claimed that many people in Alexandria and Fairfax Counties considered Burgess insane.

Governor Stuart continued to insist that there was to be no lynching. "I have saved the lives of several men and guaranteed to them the constitutional privilege of trial by jury," he insisted, hoping not to repeat the August 15, 1917 lynching of William Page near Heathsville. That was the first lynching in Virginia in 18 years.

93

Paul Langhorn

PAUL LANGHORN (also spelled Langhorne), a 49-year-old Black man from Newport News, was executed June 7, 1918, for the murder of his 14-year-old stepdaughter, Dorothy Jones.

Langhorn's motive appeared to be jealousy. According to the police, he had helped raise the girl since she was three years of age. He became obsessed with her, however, and was angered that she married a soldier and that they both lived with him and his wife.

On March 9, 1918, just after 4:00 a.m., he awakened the husband so he would make reveille at camp. After he left, Langhorn approached his daughter in bed and, declaring "she had ruined him," slashed her throat with a razor. He then went out into the yard and tried, and failed, to slash his wrist.

Police were alerted by the screams of Dorothy's mother. They arrested Langhorn and took him to the jail hospital. On March 29 he was tried in the Norfolk Corporation Court starting at 10:00 a.m. The trial was over before noon, concluding with a sentence of death.

94

Tolson Bailey

95

Guy Nixon

TWO WILMINGTON DELAWARE Black men, Tolson Bailey (age 17), and Guy Nixon (age 19) were executed in the State Penitentiary on July 2, 1918, for murdering White Norfolk gunsmith and sporting goods merchant G. Fred Dashiell on December 19, 1917.

The two men were known as "bad actors" by the Wilmington police, as they had a long history of various charges. Nixon was considered the worst of the two, having been charged in the past with housebreaking, highway robbery, and larceny.

Bailey was reported to have an obsession with stealing garden hose, which landed him in court many times. His father, Tolson Bailey Sr., had confessed to killing three men before his death years earlier.

The two men entered Dashiell's store and asked to look at some revolvers. They then asked Dashiell to load each with a bullet so they could go out back and try a target shot. After loading, Dashiell may have changed his mind and requested they pay for the pistols or hand them back. Instead of handing them back, one or both men shot him before escaping down Union Street toward Brambleton.

Hunter Sorey, a clerk, was in the store at the time but he reported the shooting happened so quickly that he had no time to stop it.

Detective Benton soon caught the men, and upon discovering the pistols arrested them both. The Norfolk Corporation Court found both men guilty of first-degree murder and sentenced them to death.

1919

96

Harvey Stuart

BUENA VISTA native Harvey Stuart was executed at the penitentiary March 26, 1919, promptly at 7:00 a.m. for the handgun murders of Monica Evelyn Leftwich and her escort, Robert Ross at a "colored dance" near Lexington in April 1918. The cause of the double murder was jealousy.

A motion of attorneys for the accused in the Circuit Court of Buena Vista to set aside the verdict as "contrary to the law and evidence" was continued until next term and the prisoner was remanded to the Lexington Jail.

On January 23, 1919, Stuart attempted a jailbreak. He muscled his way past Jailer Shoulder as he brought in food, and was almost to the front door when H. Gilmore Montgomery, a boarder with the jailer's family, intercepted him. There was a brief struggle, but Montgomery and Shoulder soon overpowered Stuart and got him back in his cell.

On March 17 the Supreme Court of Appeals denied a writ of error, and Governor Westmoreland Davis refused to intervene in the case.

Another condemned inmate, Horace Williams, immediately followed him to the chair.

97

Horace Williams

IMMEDIATELY AFTER Harvey Stuart's electrocution, Horace Williams, age 35, went to the chair on March 26, 1919, at 7:12 a.m. for the murder of Orlando T. Clark, a prominent White merchant in Mitchell, in Culpeper County.

The *Alexandria Gazette* described how Williams and an accomplice named Ernest Wilson allegedly shot and fatally wounded Clark on Thursday, February 14, 1918, in a robbery which netted them $50. Later, a .38-caliber revolver was found about 150 yards from the store, and the bullets matched the ones taken from Clark's body.

Detective Morgan Bradford arrived from Washington D.C. to investigate the killing. After suspicion pointed to Williams and Wilson, Bradford and a partner named William Sullivan confronted Wilson's common-law wife. She told Sullivan that the men had planned the robbery and murder down to "the minute details" and openly discussed how to divide the money. She then confessed that the two men had come home Thursday night, showed her a stack of bills, and threatened to kill her if she told anyone. She also stated that when she refused to leave with them, they fled west to the Blue Ridge Mountains, between Sperryville and Nethers.

Bradford told an Associated Press reporter that both men had served time at the State Penitentiary. They both were employed at a Mitchell sawmill.

Sullivan headed west, and after 48 hours caught up with the two men in a deserted cabin. He arrested them without incident and took them to jail in Mitchell. Then, after learning that "scores of Clark's friends had armed themselves," they transferred the men to

Alexandria for fears that "public opinion against the negroes was too intense" to guarantee their safety.

The February 19 trial proved that Williams was the triggerman and that he had stolen the revolver from his father. Also, Wilson had several sticks of the same brand of chewing gum in his pocket and in his home as a box that had been broken into during the robbery, proving his presence at the scene. The jury came back from deliberations with death for Williams, and life in the penitentiary for Wilson.

98

Jerry Warren

TWENTY-NINE-YEAR-OLD Black Northampton County laborer Jerry Warren was executed on June 27, 1919, at 7:40 a.m. for the November 29, 1918 handgun murder of 62-year-old White Police Sergeant James A. Taylor, of Cape Charles.

The evening before the Taylor killing, Warren shot a Black man named James Nottingham through the groin and another man, Artis Scott, in the leg during a fight over a woman at a dance. Early the next morning, a squad of sailors from the Cherrystone naval base, where Nottingham and Scott worked as cooks, fanned out in search of Warren. Sergeant Taylor led the search.

An hour later the group received word that Warren was hiding in a house in a section of town called "Negro's Rendezvous." As sailors stood guard, Taylor and Warrant Officer Ogden Lescallette entered the home. Spotting Taylor, Warren opened fire, striking the police sergeant in the arm, leg, and abdomen. He died the next day.

As Warren got away, Lescallette shot the gun from his hand, but Warren was able to pick it back up and escape the pursuing sailors, who were all chasing and firing at him.

Despite Cape Charles being guarded by a cordon of sailors and marines, Warren managed to break to Wilmington, Delaware. He was captured on December 5, however, and transported back to Virginia, where on December 19 a special session of the court tried him. Judge Fletcher sentenced him to death.

99

Emper Jacobs

ON OCTOBER 30, 1919, 29-year-old Black Portsmouth fireman Emper Jacobs was put to death at 7:15 a.m. for first-degree murder.

The previous month, on September 15, a White grocer named John Turk confronted Jacobs about an overdue grocery bill. Jacobs then allegedly shot Turk four times.

The Portsmouth Circuit Court tried, convicted, and sentenced Jacobs. The case was briefly reported only by the *Portsmouth Star* newspaper. His body was sent to the Anatomical Board at the Medical College.

1920

100

Robert Williams

TWENTY-THREE-YEAR-OLD Black Danville native Robert Williams, *alias* "Alabama red," was executed November 13, 1920, for allegedly raping a 20-year-old White woman named Annie Ross in Lynchburg. The crime occurred on August 6 as Ross walked home from the movies, and Williams was captured two days later.

The crime triggered numerous lynching attempts. On August 16, an armed mob of over 300 men stormed the Lynchburg jail in an attempt to "rescue" Williams (a code word used by lynchers), but they were held back by Jailer Tyree and a small band of deputies. After the crowd dispersed, police transferred Williams to Roanoke for safekeeping.

Then, on August 19 a mob of 25 to 50 White men gathered at 1:00 a.m. at Fort Hill, about three miles from the Roanoke Jail after the rumor circulated that Williams was going to be transferred from Roanoke back to Lynchburg. They blocked the road and even fired at one car that refused to stop after ordered to do so. The crowd considered storming the Roanoke Jail but was tipped off that the police were heavily armed and waiting for them. The *Roanoke World News* reported that day that "Feeling runs higher today than at any time since the crime and it seems certain that military protection will be necessary when Williams is returned [to Lynchburg] from Roanoke for trial."

On August 17, Judge Francis Christian, after meeting with several officers of the Corporation Court, including the commonwealth's attorney, announced he had no power to convene a special term of his court, and that Williams could not be legally tried before the term that would begin September 7. Christian could not have been happy with that determination, as he had been vacationing in Atlantic City when he was called back via telegram to provide a speedy trial for Williams, who had confessed to the rape and claimed he was ready to plead guilty.

Two young rioters, O. H. Morris and Aubrey Foster were arrested and charged with committing "unlawful assembly, route and riot" after the initial "rescue attempt" at Lynchburg. The court fined them $25 each and sentenced them to 10 days in jail.

Afterword

Electrocution Equipment and Supplies

Note: To be inspected by the Execution Team OIC or Assistant OIC

Items Checked	Condition	Checked By	Date	Time
Ammonia inhalants (1 box)				
Electric Chair				
Headpiece (natural sponge liner only)				
Leg Connection (Natural Sponge Liner Only)				
Stethoscope				
5 gallons fresh water				
3 pounds table salt				
1 fresh egg				
8 pounds ice				
10 sandbags				
Cooling Board				

_____   _____
Signature   Date

VIRGINIA DEPARTMENT OF CORRECTIONS Execution manual, Operating Procedure 460, "To establish procedures for implementing the death penalty in the Commonwealth of Virginia." Page 25. February 7, 2017. "1 fresh egg" is required supposedly to test the salinity of the salt water used to soak the sponges.

Bibliography

Annual Report(s) of the Board of Directors of the Virginia Penitentiary with Accompanying Documents. Fiscal Year(s) Ending September 30, 1900-1910.

Anonymous. "An Eyewitness Describes Death in the Electric Chair." *Richmond Times,* January 12, 1902.

Banner, Stuart. "The Death Penalty, an American History." Harvard University Press. 2002.

Bond, Gordon. "The Adams Electrical Company." (www.GardenState-Legacy.com), Issue 12, June 2011.

Brumfield, Dale M. "An Executioner's Song." *Richmond Magazine,* April, 2016.

———. "Virginia State Penitentiary: A Notorious History." Charlotte, History Press, 2017.

Carrington, Charles MD. "The History of Electrocution in the State of Virginia." Lecture transcript, 41st annual session of the Medical Society of Virginia, Norfolk, October 25-28, 1910.

Code of Virginia. Title 18.2. Crimes and Offenses Generally; Chapter 4. Crimes Against the Person; § 18.2-31. Capital murder defined; punishment.

Commonwealth of Virginia. "Report of the Virginia Penitentiary." Annual Reports of Officers, Boards, and Institutions of the Commonwealth of Virginia. Richmond, 1907-1920.

———. Annual Report(s) to the Board of Directors. Richmond: Virginia Penitentiary, 1908 -1915, 1917-1920.

———. Journal of the House of Delegates, 1908-1914, 1918-1920.

———. Journal of the Senate, "Lynchings Must Stop." 1928.

———. Report(s) of the Virginia Penitentiary. 1908-1912, 1914, 1818-1920.

———. "Senate Action on Bills." Journal of the Senate of Virginia, January 1908-1910.

———. "Senate Action on House Resolutions." Journal of the Senate of Virginia, 1908-1912.

Earley, Mark. L. "A Pink Cadillac, an IQ of 63, and a Fourteen-Year-Old from South Carolina: Why I Can No Longer Support the Death Penalty." University of Richmond Law Review 49 (2015): 811-823.

Equal Justice Initiative. "Lynching in America: Confronting the Legacy of Racial Terror." 2017.

Espy, M. Watt, John Ortiz Smykla. Executions in the United States, 1608-2016: The Espy File. Fourth Edition. Ann Arbor, MI: Inter-university Consortium for Political and Social Research, 2017.

Green, Frank. "Witnessing Executions." *University of Richmond Law Review* (2015).

Griffin, Larry J., and W. Fitzhugh Brundage. "Lynching in the New South: Georgia and Virginia, 1880-1930." *Contemporary Sociology* 23, no. 6 (1994): 814.

Grinnan, Dr. A. G. "The Burning of Eve in Virginia." *Virginia Historical Magazine*, June, 1896. (www.archive.org).

Gross, Samuel R., et al. "Race and Wrongful Convictions in the United States." The National Registry of Exonerations, Newkirk Center for Science and Society. 2017.

Hall, Randal. "A Courtroom Massacre: Politics and Public Sentiment in Progressive-Era Virginia." *Journal of Southern History,* Vol. 70, No. 2 (2004): 249-292.

Harris, LaShawn. "The 'Commonwealth of Virginia vs. Virginia Christian:' Southern Black Women, Crime & Punishment in Progressive Era Virginia." *Journal of Social History,* Vol. 47, No. 4 (2014): 922-942.

Jain, Monika. "Mitigating the Dangers of Capital Convictions Based on Eyewitness Testimony Through Treason's Two-Witness Rule," J. Crim. L. & Criminology (2000-2001): p. 761. (https://scholarlycommons.law.northwestern.edu/jclc).

Joyner, Nancy D. "The Death Penalty in Virginia: its History and Prospects." University of Virginia Institute of Government Newsletter 50, (1974): 37-40

K. M. M. and A. J. S. "Capital Punishment in Virginia." *Virginia Law Review*, Vol. 58, No. 1 (Jan. 1972), pp. 97-142.

Linders, Annulla. "The Execution Spectacle and State Legitimacy: The Changing Nature of the American Execution Audience, 1833-1937." *Law & Society Review*, vol. 36, no. 3, 2002, pp. 607–656. JSTOR, www.jstor.org/stable/1512164.

Martschukat, Jürgen. "The Art of Killing by Electricity": The Sublime and the Electric Chair." *The Journal of American History*, Vol. 89, No. 3 (Dec. 2002), pp. 900-921

Rayner, B. L. "The life of Thomas Jefferson." Boston: Lilly, Wait, Colman & Holden, 1834.

Rexroat, Barbara. Unpublished genealogy of the Seat Family, sections 3-6, 2014.

Schaikewitz, Steven and Gregory Lisby. "Harry F. Byrd and Louis Jaffe, Allies in a Just Cause: Virginia's Anti-Lynch Law of 1928." *Virginia Social Science Journal*, Vol. 43 (2008), pp. 21-37.

Scott, Ned Jr. "An Eye for an Eye: The Strange Death of Frank Coppola." *ThroTTle* Magazine. October 1982.

Shires, Carl. "Electric Chair, after 232 Executions, Loses 'Elegance'." *Richmond News Leader,* March 8, 1961.

Shuman, Edwin L. "Practical Journalism: A Complete Manual of the Best Newspaper Methods." New York, 1894.

Staff Report. "How it Feels to Die in the Electric Chair." *Richmond Times-Dispatch,* March 5, 1916.

———. "Capital Punishment—Execution By Electricity—The Kemmler Case." *Public Opinion,* April 12, 1890: pp. 432-435.

———. "Chair Claims First Woman Victim Today." *Richmond News Leader,* August 16, 1912.

———. "Christian Virginia vs. Virginia Christian," *The Crisis* Magazine, September 1912, 237–239.

———. "Die on Different Days." *Daily Press* (Newport), April 16, 1909.

———. "Extra Brutal: Kemmler Dies a Terrible Death in the Electric Chair." *The World* (New York), August 6, 1890.

———. "Finney's Sentence has been Commuted." *The Evening News* (Roanoke), October 10, 1908.

———. "Five to Die." *Roanoke Evening News,* October 6, 1908.

———. "Kemmler's Death Chair." *The Sun* (New York), April 29, 1890.

———. "Murder Confessed by Negress, Slayer of Mrs. Ida Belote." *Newport News Daily Press*, April 11, 1912.

———. "Murder of Mrs. Belote Is Deplored By Negroes." *Newport News Daily Press*, March 20, 1912.

———. "Murder of Mrs. Belote." *Hampton Monitor*, March 21, 1912.

———. "Nation Shocked by Crime at Hillsville." *Richmond Times-Dispatch*, March 29, 1913.

———. "Negro Girl Put To Death in Chair For Murdering Woman," *The Lima News,* August 16, 1912.

———. "Negro Girl Pays Death Penalty." *Richmond Times-Dispatch*, August 17, 1912.

———. "Newspaper Would Save Girl's Life." *Richmond Times-Dispatch,* August 14, 1912.

———. "No More Hangings in the Old Dominion." *The Daily Press* (Newport News), March 6, 1908.

————. "Petition for Appeal in the Christian Case." *Newport News Daily Press,* May 12, 1912.

————. "Respite Granted Young Murderess." *Richmond Times-Dispatch,* June 14, 1912

————. "Sensationalism." *The Evening News* (Roanoke), March 21, 1911.

————. "Seybold Takes Blame on his Own Shoulders." *Richmond Times-Dispatch,* January 16, 1909.

————. "Smith Sentenced." *Alexandria Gazette,* January 14, 1910.

————. "State Makes Switch to Electric Chair." Editorial, *Richmond Times-Dispatch,* April 12, 1908.

————. "The Board and its Duty." *Richmond Dispatch.* September 30, 1911.

————. "Think Electrocution of Girl Would be a Disgrace." *Richmond News Leader,* July 25, 1912.

————. "Virginia Christian Murderess, Pays Penalty of Awful Crime." *Hampton Monitor,* August 22, 1912.

————. "Young Woman Attacked by Burly Negro in Richmond, Va." *The Salt Lake Herald,* January 11, 1909.

Streib, Victor L. "Juveniles' Attitudes Toward Their Impending Executions." Excerpted from "Facing the Death Penalty." Philadelphia: Temple University Press, 1987.

Trotti, Michael A. "The Scaffold's Revival: Race and Public Execution in the South." *Journal of Social History* 45 no. 1 (2011), 195-224.

Vaughan, Charles. "Grant Me to Live: The Execution of Virginia Christian." Pittsburgh: Dorrance Publishing, 2010.

Warden, Rob and Daniel Lennard. "Death in America under Color of Law: Our Long, Inglorious Experience with Capital Punishment." Northwestern Pritzker School of Law, J. L. & Soc. Pol'y. 194 (2018). (https://scholarlycommons.law.northwestern.edu/njlsp/vol13/iss4/1).

Collections

Library of Virginia. Governor Claude Swanson executive papers, 1906-1910.

————. Governor Henry Carter Stuart executive papers, 1914-1918.

————. Governor Westmoreland Davis executive papers, 1918-1922.

————. Governor William Hodges Mann executive papers, 1910-1914.

————. Guide to the Records of the Virginia State Penitentiary.

Web and Digital Collections

Ancestry.com (https://www.ancestry.com/)

Death penalty information center (http://deathpenaltyusa.org/usa1/state/virginia)

Find a Grave Cemetery records (http://findagrave.com)

Google Scholar (https://scholar.google.com/)

HathiTrust digital library (http://hathitrust.org)

Internet Archive digital library (http://www.archive.org)

James Madison University racial terror website (https://sites.lib.jmu.edu/valynchings/)

JSTOR (https://www.jstor.org/)

Library of Congress (http://loc.gov/)

Library of congress digitized newspapers (http://chroniclingamerica.loc.gov/)

Library of Virginia online digitized newspapers (http://virginiachronicle.com)

Murderpedia encyclopedia of murderers (http://www.murderpedia.org)

Newspapers.com digitized newspapers (http://www.newspapers.com)

Virginia Center for digital history (http://www.vcdh.virginia.edu)

Virginia Heritage Guides to Manuscript and Archival Collections in Virginia (http://vaheritage.org/)

Newspapers

Alexandria Gazette	*Old Dominion Sun*
Brooklyn (NY) Daily Eagle	(Petersburg) *Progress-Index*
Clinch Valley News	*Richmond Planet*
(Fredericksburg) *Free Lance*	*Richmond Times-Dispatch*
Hampton Daily-Monitor	*Roanoke Evening News*
Leavenworth (Kansas) *Post*	*Staunton Daily Leader*
Lexington Gazette	*Staunton Dispatch-News*
Lima (Ohio) *News*	*Staunton News Leader*
Mathews Journal	*Tazewell Republican*
Newport News Daily Press	*ThroTTle*
Norfolk Journal and Guide	*Washington Post*
Norfolk Ledger-Star	*Washington Times*

Index

S

T

About the Author

Dale M. Brumfield is an anti-death penalty advocate, award-winning journalist, sometime adjunct professor, cultural archaeologist, and "American Grotesk" historyteller. Dale received his MFA in fiction from Virginia Commonwealth University in 2015 and has been published in numerous publications nationwide. He is the author of 11 books, including "Virginia State Penitentiary: A Notorious History."

Special thanks to the incredible Susan, and the greatest kids in the world, Hunter, Jackson, and Hollis.

#Americangrotesk

#11years11books

www.dalebrumfield.net

Lightning Source UK Ltd.
Milton Keynes UK
UKHW010815080222
398361UK00001B/123